TAROT OF THE
Enchanted Soul

YASMEEN WESTWOOD

Copyright © 2022 by Yasmeen Westwood

Library of Congress Control Number: 2021931778

All rights reserved. No part of this work may be reproduced or used in any form or by any means—graphic, electronic, or mechanical, including photocopying or information storage and retrieval systems—without written permission from the publisher.

The scanning, uploading, and distribution of this book or any part thereof via the Internet or any other means without the permission of the publisher is illegal and punishable by law. Please purchase only authorized editions and do not participate in or encourage the electronic piracy of copyrighted materials.

"Red Feather Mind Body Spirit" logo is a trademark of Schiffer Publishing, Ltd.
"Red Feather Mind Body Spirit Feather" logo is a registered trademark of Schiffer Publishing, Ltd.

Designed by Danielle D. Farmer
Cover design by Danielle D. Farmer
Type set in Desire/Fenice BT/Minion Pro

ISBN: 978-0-7643-6281-1
Printed in China

Published by REDFeather Mind, Body, Spirit
An imprint of Schiffer Publishing, Ltd.
4880 Lower Valley Road
Atglen, PA 19310
Phone: (610) 593-1777; Fax: (610) 593-2002
E-mail: Info@redfeathermbs.com
Web: www.redfeathermbs.com

For our complete selection of fine books on this and related subjects, please visit our website at www.redfeathermbs.com. You may also write for a free catalog.

REDFeather Mind, Body, Spirit's titles are available at special discounts for bulk purchases for sales promotions or premiums. Special editions, including personalized covers, corporate imprints, and excerpts, can be created in large quantities for special needs. For more information, contact the publisher.

We are always looking for people to write books on new and related subjects. If you have an idea for a book, please contact us at proposals@schifferbooks.com.

Do not let your fire go out, spark by irreplaceable spark in the hopeless swamps of the not-quite, the not-yet, and the not-at-all. Do not let the hero in your soul perish in lonely frustration for the life you deserved and have never been able to reach.

The world you desire can be won.
It exists . . . it is real . . . it is possible . . . it's yours.

Dedicated to an Enchanted Soul...

My husband David, father to Arran and stepdad to Amber and Aaliyah. Hope you have found what you were forever searching for . . . Rest in Peace.

Welcome	9
Introduction	10
The Major Arcana Explanation	14
The Minor Arcana Explanation	16
The Court Cards Explanation	17
Beginning a Reading	18
Learning the Cards	20
Basic Tarot Spreads	21
3-Card Spread	21
4-Card Love Spread	22
5-Card Spread	23
7-Card Relationship Spread	24
10-Card Celtic Cross Spread	26
12-Card Astrological Spread	28
16-Card General Spread	30
The Major Arcana	32
The Suit of Cups	78
The Suit of Swords	94
The Suit of Wands	110
The Suit of Coins	126
Acknowledgments	142

Welcome

Welcome to the *Tarot of the Enchanted Soul* and the guidebook on how to understand and read the Tarot cards. Tarot has been gaining in popularity over the years as more and more people look toward personal self-development and are more open to exploring the unseen. Being a Tarot reader no longer carries the negative connotations it did in the past.

The purpose of this guidebook, apart from explaining the meanings of each card, is to help you use Tarot as a tool for self-development, to help you understand yourself better. Tarot works by tapping into your intuition, a very powerful inner voice, which if you listen to it can help you with life decisions and also assist in times of uncertainty. We ALL have the power to access this intuition. No special powers or abilities are required to do so. The Tarot is a tool to help you find and utilize this inner voice.

The guidebook has been written in a format that will allow you to journal as you work through the cards. Each card contains a question for you to ponder, as well as an affirmation and a task to do relating to the card. So, the more honest you are in answering the questions, the more you will begin to find out who you are, and using the cards daily will help sharpen your intuition until you are able to recognize and listen to it without having to try.

For me, Tarot is like a dreamworld, a place where magic happens, and I am so excited to bring this dreamworld to you. Creating this deck has been and is a wonderful journey involving a lot of fun (and tears), and with each card I have put in a little bit of myself. So welcome to the *Tarot of the Enchanted Soul* . . . and let the magic begin!

Lots of love,

Introduction

What Is the Tarot?

Tarot cards have been around since the fourteenth century and appear to have originated in Europe. The oldest surviving set is called the Tarocchi in Italian and appears to date from 1420 to 1450. Some people believe that the cards originated in ancient Egypt, and the common myth is that Tarot was brought to Europe by gypsies.

Tarot cards have frequently been used as a tool for fortune-telling or divination and have also been used in one form or another for understanding the self and the world. So, it's no wonder that in this time of chaos in the world, Tarot seems to be growing in popularity!

In the past, and even now, people who interpreted the cards were given great power and held in reverence as great fortune-tellers, and this seems to be the case today, with people believing the interpretation as "the truth" as exactly what is going to happen and that nothing can be done to change it. However, I believe that little in our lives is fixed, and we can influence and change most things in our lives—but only if we choose to take responsibility for our own lives.

Misconceptions of Tarot

Unfortunately, there are some people who seem to have a negative view of the Tarot cards; they think they are the work of the devil or some sort of black magic, People assume that if you can read the Tarot, then it means you can delve deep into their minds and know all their deepest and darkest secrets! That is definitely not the case. There are, however, other misconceptions made about the Tarot by people who have never used it:

1. Tarot can tell you EVERYTHING! The Tarot does not tell you 100 percent categorically what is going to happen in your life; only YOU have complete control over what happens in your life. The Tarot cannot tell you what decisions to make; it can help you look at things you may not have considered. But at the end of the day, you are the one who can make the choice and feel the consequences arising from it. You cannot blame the Tarot if the outcome is not what you expected, based on a decision YOU made. Most importantly (and this scares loads of people), the Tarot is very unlikely to predict death.

2. Tarot is something to fear! There is nothing to fear with Tarot. It is made up of picture cards, which are open to YOUR interpretation. Someone else may look at the exact same image and interpret it in a totally different way. Also, you may look at the same card another day and see something entirely different. Tarot is not associated with any religion, cult, devil, or voodoo, or any other sinister thing.

3. Tarot requires psychic skills! Not true. You do not have to have any special skills, nor do you need to be a clairvoyant, medium, or psychic to be able to work with the cards. Anyone can "read" the cards. All you are doing is telling a story based on what the images show. We all possess natural psychic skills, and sometimes using the cards on a daily basis can open up these skills.

There are just a few of the misconceptions people have of Tarot. Are there any other misconceptions or rules you've heard of? What are they?

Choosing a Tarot Deck

Many people ask me how to choose a Tarot deck. Well, what I do is look at new decks that are available on Amazon, Google, or other venues. These sites always have images of decks, and I look at what imagery "speaks" to me. Some decks resonate very strongly, while others do not at all. It's very important to look at decks, since you need the cards to be able to "talk" to you. I have found that when I love the imagery, then it's very easy to interpret the cards rather than struggle with interpretation of cards whose images you really do not like.

Storing Tarot Cards

Traditionally, Tarot cards are stored in a silk cloth—silk protects from negative energies. There are many ways in which you can protect your cards from negative energies and to ensure they are not damaged: a silk scarf, wooden box, tin box, cloth, etc.

Cleaning Your Tarot Cards

Tarot cards need to be cleaned occasionally to remove any residual energies, especially when people have been shuffling and handling the cards a lot. This can be done in a number of ways. Again, choose what you feel comfortable with. I tend to cleanse my cards by using incense. You can use

- smudging with sage or incense (or both)
- crystals
- Reiki

For more information about cleansing and other similar applications, one good resource is www.biddytarot.com.

Ethics of Reading

Know that you have responsibilities when you read for others. Readings must be done with the intention of helping the person who has come to you for a reading, NOT for enhancing your ego or for you to use that information in a negative way against a person. It is completely unethical and extremely irresponsible to predict anyone's death. NEVER EVER do that! If you see tough times ahead for someone, then it is best to talk about any problems or challenges ahead rather than a black-and-white reading.

Do NOT make decisions for another; by all means give advice and get them to see what they need to do, but do not offer any unsolicited advice, since it could come back and bite you!

Always remember to inform people that there is NO guarantee regarding any prediction, and that they make their own choices. Do not play doctor, and never make a judgment or diagnosis about any ill health, since you are not a medical practitioner.

Respect at all times the free will of every human, and keep yourself centered in love and light. Remember that we are all divine in essence. Do not judge; seek understanding.

How Can Tarot Help?

Tarot can do the following:

1. Help you tap into your own intuition and inner wisdom, so you can "know" with accuracy when something is right for you. It can also help validate your own feelings as to what the next steps are for you.

2. Help you see light at the end of the tunnel when you are surrounded in darkness and life feels hopeless. The Tarot may help by bringing in hope, optimism, and encouragement to your life. Sometimes that is enough to open up to your own creativity, problem solving, and intuition and the ability to notice a different way forward.

3. Help you if you have a difficult choice to make, by helping you safely explore various options before you rush in and commit yourself to something that you may later regret.

4. Help by showing you the energies around you and indicating what may be blocking you from having the success you deserve or from moving forward. Often the Tarot can assist to show you the ways to overcome the blocks, by asking you probing questions.

What other ways do you think the Tarot can help?

The Major Arcana
EXPLANATION

A standard Tarot deck consists of 78 cards divided into two parts: the Major and Minor Arcana. There are 22 cards in the Major Arcana, from the Fool (0) to the World (XXI or 21). There are 56 cards in the Minor Arcana, divided into four suits. For each suit, the cards are numbered Ace to Ten, and there are four Court cards (Page, Knight, Queen, and King). These 22 cards of the Major Arcana symbolize some universal aspect of human experience.

If you see a lot of Major Arcana cards in a reading or a spread, then it is likely that those issues are very important issues in the person's life and that the impact of the situations may well be there for some time. They cover virtually every aspect of someone's life. It can also be seen as the journey through life or a more spiritual journey, and the lessons that need to be learned, since they point to some major lessons or qualities we need to find in ourselves to be able to move forward with a situation and, often, with our lives.

Some say that the Major Arcana show the different stages on a individual's journey of inner growth, in what some call the Fool's Journey—a journey to self-realization, and that we all travel through life, complete with detours, backups, and restarts.

The Minor Arcana
EXPLANATION

The rest of the deck is made up of four suits called the Minor Arcana, representing the day-to-day nature of life, These can be compared to the suits in a deck of playing cards.

The first is the **Suit of Cups**, which usually represents emotions and feelings—the dreamy, emotional aspects of our life—and has to do with relationships. So, we have the beginning of a relationship (Ace of Cups) all the way to the happy family (Ten of Cups). Astrologically they represent the element of Water and the signs of Cancer, Scorpio, and Pisces.

The next is the **Suit of Swords**, which is the Suit of the Mind: our thoughts, our worries, our concerns, and matters of knowledge, and they point toward mental activity and head stuff with thoughts, ideas, fears, and logic. Swords represent the element of Air and the astrological signs of Gemini, Libra, and Aquarius.

Then we have the **Suit of Wands**: our creativity, ambitions, and decisions in the world. The Wands refer to matters having to do with action, work, career, business, creativity, moving forward. Wands are represented by the element of Fire and represent the zodiac signs of Aries, Leo, and Sagittarius.

Last, we have the **Suit of Coins**, which are all about the material things in life, be it money, resources, or your time. They show us all the different stages of financial issues. Coins represent the element of Earth and the astrological signs of Taurus, Virgo, and Capricorn.

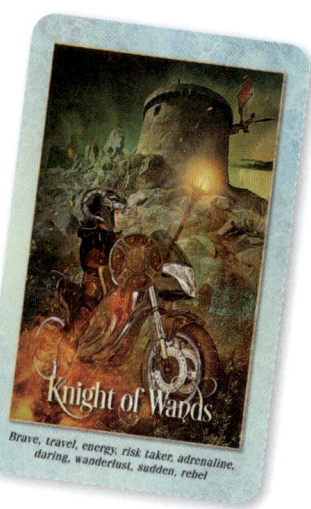

The Court Cards
EXPLANATION

The Court cards can indicate people with certain character traits, as well as emotions that people may experience.

The Page. The Pages in a suit represent new beginnings or some message being offered to you—something with the potential to change you.

The Knight. The Knights are all about action and bravery. They are also known for their impulsiveness and about *doing* something as opposed to waiting for something to happen *to* you.

The Queen. The Queen in a suit is about nurturing, compassion, intuition, and protection. The Queen has mastered the traits of the suit in which she is found.

The King. The King is all about success, control, mastery, wisdom, and fairness. The King shows the characteristics of maturity of its suit and, like the Queen, has mastered all there is to know about the suit, and as such can use his wisdom to counsel others.

Beginning a Reading

Step 1: Set the mood

The first step is to relax your mind and to ground yourself. So, make yourself comfortable, listen to meditative music, or burn incense. I tend to burn incense to help me open up my intuition and imagine roots coming out of my feet, going deep into the ground, to help me ground, since I can find I get "spacey" otherwise. Clear your mind and release any tension in your body, because if you are tense, then you will not be relaxed enough to do the reading.

Step 2: Shuffle the cards

You need to shuffle your cards, since they may still be in the previous reading order. To ensure you are starting with a clear deck, shuffle your cards, imagining clear light bathing the cards. It is important to shuffle the cards because this is how you sort through all the forms your reading could take, and arrange at a subtle level the card you will receive.

Step 3: Ask the question

Holding your deck, ask the question in your head. How you ask the question is important. A reading may be completely general, directed toward a particular area of concern or performed to address a specific question. Instead of a type of question with a clear yes or no answer, consider asking what you need to know from the cards regarding a particular situation, or what the message for the day is.

Step 4: Select your cards

One way to choose is to place your Tarot deck in front of you and, using your left hand, cut the deck in half and place the top half on the left. You should have two piles of cards now. Choose the card that is on the top of the right pile, and turn it over. This is just a guide, and you may have your own way of selecting cards. I do not cut the deck. Whenever I shuffle, cards tend to jump out, and those are the ones that I select. There is no right or wrong way in which to select your cards.

Step 5: Create the spread

A spread is a pattern for laying out the cards. It defines how many cards to use, where each one goes, and what each one means. A spread is a template guiding the placement of the cards so they can shed light on a given topic. There are many, many different types of spreads, and some of the more common ones are listed in the forthcoming pages. Choose your cards as in the shuffling technique in step 4 and lay them out in front of you as per the spread chosen. Pick all cards before turning them over for an interpretation.

Step 6: Interpret the reading

For the actual reading you may want to keep a pen and paper handy to record what comes up during the reading, or to record it as a voice clip. Do not censor what comes up—be honest and let it flow. These are the things to look out for:

- What is the name of the card?
- Describe the card; what do you see on it? It may be literal or your impression. What is going on in the card? Is it an action card or a card where nothing much is happening? Who is in the card? Why do you think they are there?
- What are the symbols on the card? Describe the image, colors, numbers, or words that catch your attention. What do the colors mean to you? What do the symbols mean?
- What is the mood of the card? How does this card make you feel? Do you like the feeling of it, or does the mood make you want to put it away?
- What does this card make you think of? Does it remind you of an event or someone from your life? Notice your first impressions and your emotional reaction to it. Why do you think you have had that emotional reaction?
- What else stands out?
- If you were in the card, what story would it be telling you?

Step 7: Closing the reading

When you feel it is time to end the Tarot reading, write down the cards you selected and their positions. It is easy to forget them—especially if you have a memory like mine! Then, clear the deck to remove all traces of the energy patterns of this reading; this can be done by scrambling the cards together gently.

Before putting the cards away, hold your deck in your hands and silently thank it for all the insights and guidance it has brought to you this day. Express your gratitude to your Inner Guide for helping you via the Tarot cards.

Learning the Cards

Keeping a Tarot Journal

A Tarot journal is a place where you can record your personal thoughts, insights, observations, and notes about each of the cards to help expand your Tarot knowledge and skills. The journal can also include Tarot readings that you have done, spreads you have used or created, and your own notes about each card. The journal can be either a notebook you have personalized or have created as an electronic format, or any medium that you feel comfortable with.

Perhaps one of the most common methods for learning the cards with a Tarot journal is to use the Card-a-Day exercise, where you can use your journal to record your thoughts on an individual Tarot card drawn for each day. That is what I used to do when I was learning about the decks, rather than trying to remember every single card in one go. Capture the aspects we looked at above, and you will find that you form your own meanings for each of the cards. Each card will mean something to YOU. Assign people you know with the characteristics of the card, since this makes it easier to remember. I've done that and found it to be quite fun! Don't be surprised if you can't remember all of them straight away. Learn the keywords associated with each card—if you like—and it can be helpful to imagine each card as a character in a story... What story would it tell you? Note this in your journal.

The more you use your cards, the quicker you will learn, and they will become familiar to you. And you may find that they begin to talk to you as soon as you pick them up!

Basic Tarot Spreads

The following are basic Tarot spreads to help you begin your Tarot journey. As you become more and more familiar with the different spreads, you may consider adjusting these or consider creating your own spreads.

1. 3-Card Spread
2. 4-Card Love Spread
3. 5-Card Spread
4. 7-Card Relationship Spread
5. 10-Card Celtic Cross Spread
6. 12-Card Astrological Spread
7. 16-Card General Spread

3-CARD SPREAD

This Tarot spread is a quick and simple way to get insight into the past, present, and future. If you need clarification on any of the positions and meanings, you can always draw an extra card.

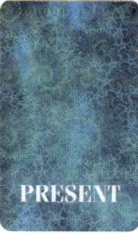

4-CARD LOVE SPREAD

This is a good spread to use if you are looking for insight into a romantic relationship. You can use it to check out your physical, mental, and spiritual/emotional connections with your other half.

Card 1: Physical connection
The physical (sex and intimacy; physical attraction)

Card 2: Mental connections
Similar interests and communication

Card 3: Spiritual/emotional connection
Shared goals, dreams, and love; mutual respect for each other

Card 4: Long-term potential of relationship

5-CARD SPREAD

This Tarot spread gives a quick answer or answers to some very basic problems and concerns. The spread can be repeated multiple times to represent different facets of a problem.

Card 1: Present position
How have you arrived at the point you are now?

Card 2: Present expectations
What are your expectations now?

Card 3: The unexpected
What is being hidden from you at the moment but may happen?

Card 4: Immediate future
What will be arriving shortly? (it could be people, events, etc.)

Card 5: Long-term future
What is the long-term future?

7-CARD RELATIONSHIP SPREAD

This spread can give you some important insight into the inner workings of your relationship, including challenges, hopes, dreams, needs, and wants, guiding you toward deeper communication and understanding.

Card 1: Your personality

Card 2: Your partner's personality

Card 3: Your challenges/blocks (challenges you bring into the relationship)

Card 4: Your partner's challenges/blocks (challenges they bring into the relationship)

Card 5: Your hopes and dreams

Card 6: Your partner's hopes and dreams

Card 7: What connects you? (what it is that brings you together)

10-CARD CELTIC CROSS SPREAD

The 10-card Celtic Cross spread is the most commonly used layout for reading the cards. It gives an overview of the past, present, and future. There are many different versions of the Celtic Cross spread, so please feel free to add your twist to it if you wish.

Card 1: Situation now

Card 2: What's helping/hindering

Card 3: Subconscious influence

Card 4: Past

Card 5: Conscious desires

Card 6: Immediate focus

Card 7: How you see yourself

Card 8: How others see you

Card 9: Hopes/fears

Card 10: Final outcome

CARD 5

CARD 4 CARD 2 CARD 6 CARD 10
        CARD 1   CARD 9

CARD 4   CARD 8

                        CARD 7

12-CARD ASTROLOGICAL SPREAD

This spread can also be used to represent the 12 houses of a person's life in astrology. It is useful to gain more information into a particular area. Again, you an add more cards to each house for more detail.

What is a house? You may have seen a birth chart and wondered why it looks like a pizza cut into 12 slices.

The houses refer to different areas of the sky, and astrologically there are 12 houses in a birth chart; each symbolizes 12 categories of life where the action of your life takes place, or challenges that you may face along the way. The first house is always located at the position where the hour hand is at one o'clock on the face of a clock. The rest of the houses are lined up going in a counterclockwise direction on the zodiac wheel.

Understanding the houses of the chart can help you understand where you are comfortable, where you find challenge, and where the dramas of your life take place.

House 1: The self (our personality and how others see us)

House 2: Money and possessions

House 3: Communication as well as day-to-day activities

House 4: Home life, ancestry, siblings, family, parents

House 5: Pleasure, romance, parties, children, affairs, creativity

House 6: Work and health, both emotional and physical

House 7: Partnerships, both personal and professional, marriage

House 8: Legacies, the occult, sex, death, transformations

House 9: Spiritual, religion, education, travel, philosophy

House 10: Career, profession, authority, fame, reputation

House 11: Friends, groups, organizations, hopes and dreams

House 12: Fears, enemies, the unseen, subconscious, restrictions, dangers

16-CARD GENERAL SPREAD

This 16-card general spread gives us a good overall impression of what's going on with a person physically, emotionally, mentally, and spiritually. It shows us the potential for the next 12 months and highlights any problem areas that may need addressing. I love this spread and have used it many, many times.

Cards 1 and 2: The past and how it affects what is going on now

Cards 3 and 4: The present

Cards 5 and 6: What the person desires

Card 7: Focus area

Card 8: What needs to be avoided

Cards 9 and 10: Next 3 months

Cards 11 and 12: Next 3–6 months

Cards 13 and 14: Next 6–9 months

Cards 15 and 16: Next 9–12 months

CARD 1	CARD 2	CARD 3	CARD 4
CARD 5	CARD 6	CARD 7	CARD 8
CARD 9	CARD 10	CARD 11	CARD 12
CARD 13	CARD 14	CARD 15	CARD 16

The Major Arcana

0. The Fool — Innocence, freedom, new adventure, leap of faith, wonder, naivete

I. The Magician — Resourcefulness, action, manifestation, mastery, skill, focus, alchemy

II. The High Priestess — Intuition, sacred wisdom, secrets, subconscious, mind

III. The Empress — Nurturing, fertility, pregnancy, creativity, sensuality, abundance

IV. The Emperor — Discipline, structure, rules, authority, fatherhood, leadership, stability

V. The Mentor — Blind faith, guide, religious beliefs, conformity, rituals, ceremonies

VI. The Lovers — Desire, relationships, choice, passion, union, romance

VII. The Chariot — Victory, success, willpower, control, forward movement, force, ambition

VIII. Strength — Bravery, patience, pride, determination, courage, endurance, compassion

IX. The Hermit — Loneliness, solitude, inspiration, introspection, stillness, contemplation, meditation

Fortune, luck, destiny, karma, fate, opportunity, randomness, change

Justice, balance, fairness, impartiality, legal matters, wisdom

Perspective, limbo, sacrifice, letting go, surrender, enlightenment, delay, reflection, insight

Endings, beginnings, transition, transformation, regeneration, renewal, rebirth

Balance, harmony, calm, serenity, peace, healing, diplomacy, moderation

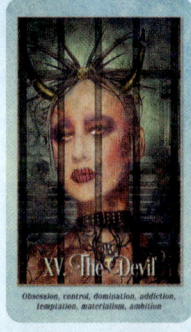

Obsession, control, domination, addiction, temptation, materialism, ambition

Upheaval, disgrace, calamity, release, downfall, flash of insight, revelation

Renewal, hope, inspiration, serenity, calm, wishes, dreams, healing, miracles

Mystery, subconscious, secrecy, illusion, fear, phobias, paranoia, obsession

Success, enlightenment, joy, happiness, child, sadness, industry

Judgment, rebirth, awakening, resurrection, inner calling, transformation

Completion, wholeness, attainment, fulfilment, triumph, end of a cycle

0 The Fool

I don't know what we're doing here—you and me . . . I don't know what we are or what we can be, but this doesn't have to be about that. This can just be about . . . a chance. Taking a chance . . .
—Dianna Hardy

KEYWORDS

Innocence, freedom, new adventure, leap of faith, wonder, naivete

Once upon a time, during a full moon, a girl—young and naive—decided to go for a walk in the woods. She was having trouble sleeping, feeling unsettled. For a long time now, she had felt as if there was something missing in her life. Was there more? The woods were dark and scary in the night, and she was glad she had her companion—Wolf—with her. He went everywhere with her. She felt safe when he was around. Not that she was scared or anything, since she was way too brave for that (or so she told herself!), but it was nice to have someone to talk to. As they hiked through the dark, dense woods, they came across a path. She had never seen it before. It had stone steps leading up to an open book, covered in climbing roses.

"How strange?" she thought. An owl sat on top of the book, flapping its wings. It was beckoning her to walk forward. Great big yellow butterflies flew in and out of the book, and in the distance, she could see a rainbow and a sunlit path, leading further into the book. "Wow! How exciting," she exclaimed and clapped her hands in glee. "I wonder where this path goes?" Nothing exciting ever happened to her, and she was not going to pass on an opportunity right in front of her. Who knows . . . maybe Narnia existed up the steps. Now wouldn't that be a story to tell? She had a feeling the steps would lead her to a wonderful story. Her mind was made up. She was going to follow the path and see where it led. Never mind the fact that she had not packed anything for the journey. She was hesitant to go back home and pack a case. What if the path disappeared by the time she got back, and it just vanished, never to appear again? No. Darn the consequences, she was going now! Maybe she was a naive fool, but she had a feeling that an exciting adventure awaited her. She had to be brave and take the risk. With a feeling of excitement and a fear of the unknown, she stepped forward onto the stone steps. Home could wait, for now.

MEANING

Like the girl in the story, how many times have you been presented with an opportunity but you have not acted on it? This card is about taking a chance. You may not have a clue where you are going; maybe there is a strong feeling that you need to go somewhere. Trust in the universe. Let it take you. This is a new and exciting beginning. Know that you are protected on this journey, and take the first step to writing your own story. What will that story be?

PERSON

The Fool person is someone who, although it may not necessarily be someone young in age, is certainly young and naive in outlook. They see possibilities and tend to follow their heart, taking a chance without weighing the consequences of the risk. They have the innocent notion that faith in an endeavor will be enough to see them through. Their approach to life can be on the unconventional side, and they may come across as rebellious and unwilling to settle down, unable to fulfill responsibilities as they go off on yet another adventure. The Fool person can be too trusting, and this may be taken advantage of by others who would seek to exploit their naivete for their own gains. They love to travel and can be the life and soul of the party!

THOUGHTS

How often do you take risks in life? What stops you from following your dreams?

I
The Magician

Manifestation is a process by which we transform seemingly unrealizable imaginations to reality.
—Debasish Mridha

KEYWORDS

Resourcefulness, action, manifestation, mastery, skill, focus, alchemy

Once upon a time there was a magician. He loved being able to do magic and especially loved teaching others what he knew. He had trained for many years to perfect his craft. Today, he had an audience of new apprentices and was teaching them about the power of manifestation. Focus was important—he told them—and for that they needed to ensure they were in control of their mind, body, soul, and emotions. To manifest what you wanted required needing to be very clear and specific about what it is that they wanted to create. He carried on explaining. A wishy-washy mind that constantly changed its desires is never going to get anyone anything! It's important to be emotionally strong. If the emotions were constantly up and down, then that was a distraction to focusing. The body required exercise and self-care. There was a reason for the mantra "healthy body, healthy mind." How can anyone focus and concentrate if they are exhausted! And finally, trusting the universe and feeling connected to it. It is the universe that holds all that we desire and brings it to us, once we are in alignment with it. If any disconnect whatsoever between the Soul and the universe is felt, then we lose access to the magic and lose the ability to harness the powerful energy for creating. Meditation, he said, was one way of helping people access the magic of the universe.

He then began to focus on the space in front of him, not wavering for even a second. The air began to swirl and a blue mist appeared, out of which a small red dragon appeared, hovering in nothing. It looked him in the eyes, before disappearing. The magician smiled and looked at his wide-eyed students "Now that's magic . . . or is it?"

MEANING

You have all that is required to manifest that which your heart desires. Be clear on what that is. Pay attention to your mind, emotions, body, and soul. Are they all in sync and functioning to ensure you can create what you want? Be aware of things being too good to be true and that you are not being shown an illusion.

PERSON

The Magician person is someone who is charming, confident, charismatic, and a great communicator. They can charm you with the gift of gab, and before you know it you are under their spell! They tend to be very highly motivated and can be extremely focused on the end goal. When they are given a task, they can seem to magic resources out of thin air and accomplish the task without much effort. They have an uncanny way of turning ideas into reality and are endowed with clear thinking and communication. The Magician personality may also be controlling and manipulating, in a very subtle way, and turn to deception when it suits them, and may do whatever it takes to get their desires.

THOUGHTS

Which area(s) do you feel you need to work on? Mind, body, soul, or emotions? Today, look at how your internal chatter can cause you to abandon something you desire. How will you silence it?

II
The High Priestess

You have to leave the city of your comfort and go into the wilderness of your intuition. What you'll discover will be wonderful. What you'll discover is yourself.

—Alan Alda

KEYWORDS

Intuition, sacred wisdom, secrets, subconscious, mind

Once upon a time there was a woman who was beautiful, yet with an air of shadowy mystery about her. She would watch, patiently, as people sought answers to the many questions they had. Who am I? What is my purpose? Why am I here? What are my talents? That was just the start! If only they would quiet down and listen. That's all they needed to do. She would whisper to them but she could not help them, unless they were aware she was there. They just needed to quiet down and reach deep into themselves, where she resided, and they would find all that they were looking for. Many centuries she had traveled and gathered much knowledge along the way—knowledge that was there for them to use as they wished. A few of them did listen to her and were able to access the secret knowledge she held—well, some of it at least. Of course, she wouldn't give it ALL away. I mean, she wasn't going to do all the work for them, but she was able to reveal a part of the answer to those who came seeking. She could help them with decisions they spent ages agonizing over. She was a part of them. She was their intuition and carried all the knowledge they needed. Only if they quieted themselves and listened to their instincts, instead of listening to the lies around them. That was how she worked. She spoke to them through instincts and dreams, through metaphysical tools and powerful feelings. She would reveal secret, hidden paths, shining a light on them, for those who sought the knowledge. For those who saw her.

MEANING

Have you been listening to your intuition? What decisions do you have that you are struggling with? This card is about quieting the mind and listening to you instincts. What do they tell you? You already know the answers. Sometimes we may not have all the information in hand, and receiving this card can indicate that some knowledge is still hidden from you. Do not make any hasty decisions. Wait until you have all the information you need. Listen to your dreams and meditate so that you are more in tune with your inner voice.

PERSON

The High Priestess person is someone who is wise and able to keep secrets. They will help you when you need advice, and assist you when you need to find your intuition. The High Priestess people contain much wisdom, which they are willing to share with those who come seeking. They are very aware of their intuition and trust it implicitly, which gives them an uncanny ability to see through someone's hidden agenda. Because they are so sure of their own ability, they may come across as quite intimidating to others, who worry about how much of their deepest, darkest secrets are not hidden to this person. It's almost as if the High Priestess can download your entire secrets within minutes of meeting you! They may know all your secrets, but they will never judge you for what lies in your subconscious, and they will never use the information against you. They are quite compassionate individuals who have a great understanding of human nature, which they are willing to share with others. Some High Priestess persons may come across as quite aloof and may be subject to bouts of depression or mood swings.

THOUGHTS

When faced with a decision, where do you seek answers? Pay attention to things around you, such as numbers, songs, feelings, and even dreams. What messages are all these bits of information giving you? Do they help with any decisions you have been struggling to make recently?

III
The Empress

Fertility is all about giving birth, over and over again!
—Petra Hermans

KEYWORDS

Nurturing, fertility, pregnancy, creativity, sensuality, abundance

Once upon a time there was a person who had an idea. That idea filled them with passion, and oh how much they wanted it to be brought to reality. As they wandered, they thought about the shortcuts they might take to make the idea come to life. Soon enough they came across a woman unlike any other they had ever seen before. She wore a crown of greenery and a silver, shimmery moon, from which smaller moons dangled. These represented the seasons of the year. Her long, pale-blonde hair caressed her pregnant bump. She was no ordinary woman—she was the keeper of an idea, incubating it, allowing it to come forth when the time was ready. People were impatient—they wanted everything now, and she had advice for the person who stood before her. She could sense their frustration. She gently reminded them, that all seeds, whether they were ideas, creativity, dreams, or even babies, needed time to grow. And in order to grow, they needed to be nurtured. A seed does not suddenly grow into a tree overnight, does it? It requires time, energy, patience, dedication—things that nurture a seed until it is ready to blossom. All the things without which there would be no growth, since the seed would be neglected and die. Many moons may pass, from planting the seed to it becoming a mature tree. We do not see what is going on during this gestation period, but we need to trust that everything will be ready when it is time to come forth. There is no need to worry and fret. She, the Empress, would hold the space during this incubation period. She was a fertile womb in which many seeds had been planted, grown, and thrived. The person understood what they needed to do. They needed to trust in the process of each stage of bringing their idea to life.

MEANING

What new venture or dream are you thinking of birthing? This is the time to plant those seeds of ideas and to keep nurturing those ideas. Like it takes a baby nine months to develop, allow patience as you watch your ideas grow until they are fully developed. This is not the time to rush anything. This card is about nurturing yourself and others. Make sure you do no spend all your time mothering others, at the cost of your own self. This is an excellent card with regard to fertility matters and can represent pregnancy or birth.

PERSON

The Empress person is the deeply compassionate, ultimate mother figure. The person is creative, sensual, and warm and has a very kind nature. They tend to live a very fulfilled life. People are drawn to this person, for the Empress loves to help others—whether it's feeding, listening, or nurturing. They tend to be very empathic and can sometimes end up looking after everyone else, to the detriment of their own self and needs. They see beauty in life in their waking moments. Everything is beauty and deserves compassion. They are natural nurturers and they love to express themselves in a creative manner. However, because they can spend too much time looking after everyone else, they may not have the time for creative expression, which may lead to frustration and exhaustion. People-pleasing may be something they do just to make everyone happy, and as a result this may lead to them to feel as if they have lost their identity in the people they are nurturing.

THOUGHTS

How much of your time is spent nurturing yourself? Do you give too much of yourself to others and neglect yourself? Spend some time outdoors in Mother Nature and connect with yourself.

IV
The Emperor

Only he who has no use for the empire is fit to be entrusted with it.
—Zhuangzi

KEYWORDS

Discipline, structure, rules, authority, fatherhood, leadership, stability

Once upon a time there was an emperor who looked out onto his kingdom. He looked at all the soldiers who stood before him, ready to go into battle upon his command. They did not question his authority, and they followed his rules. As he sat on the edge of the window, looking onto the plains below, he thought back to a time when he was a boy; his father had been a very tough emperor who had implemented many rules and regulations, which he had expected his kingdom to follow. Rules upon rules he thrust upon his people, until the power had driven him mad. He had been known as the Mad Emperor and lost his power. As a young boy the son of the Mad Emperr had witnessed how power had the capacity to corrupt. Since then he had been determined to be a just and wise emperor when it was his turn.

As he sat alone, the emperor heard a voice. Sitting perched on his shoulder was a green dragon. Was it real? Or was it his inner conscience? Either way, the dragon with his fangs and yellow eyes—which screamed rage and destruction—was a stark contrast to the emperor's now-guilt-ridden eyes masked by regret and disdain. Had he gone too far in his quest for power? To him, like his father before him, the need for rules, discipline, and structure was imperative to maintain HIS great kingdom. He had started off being a just and wise emperor, but the people saw him as too soft. Had he wanted to take back the power his father had lost control of to ensure that history would not repeat itself? He had wanted the people to follow his rules; he was in charge. He believed he was right—in fact, he knew he was, but the dragon settled on his shoulder made him feel uneasy. He had birthed a vicious tyrant, and he knew that the dragon was here to stay.

MEANING

The Emperor card is about rules and structure. It's about implementing discipline in whatever area of your life requires it. Where do you feel you lack power, or maybe you have too much power over someone or something? Are you making sure that you are not using your power to control others? With great power comes great responsibility, someone once said. How are you using your power over others? Are they allowed to be themselves, or must they follow your way?

PERSON

The Emperor person is someone who is authoritative and loves to be in charge. They give the orders and are the leaders rather than the followers. They have usually worked hard to reach their position of leadership and do not like being told "no." Highly assertive and confident, they are possessive of their little world, be it the family or work. It is their world and, therefore, their rules. Rules are very important to the Emperor person, and they will follow them religiously and expect others to do the same. They are reliable and stable but can be quite aloof and hard to get to know, since they are not prone to grand displays of emotions. They love power and can become too controlling in an effort to make sure things are done in the way they think is the "right" way, because, don't you know . . . their way is the only way and it's the right way!

THOUGHTS

Think of an example of something you are wanting to do (or wanted to achieve), and it isn't working. Why do you think that is? Do you have concrete plans in place to achieve it? What goals can you set for yourself along the way, and how will you monitor those goals?

Blind faith, guide, religious beliefs, conformity, rituals, ceremonies

V
The Mentor

But merely being tradition does not make something worthy, Kadash. We can't just assume that because something is old it is right.

—Brandon Sanderson

KEYWORDS

Blind faith, guide, religious beliefs, conformity, rituals, ceremonies

Once upon a time there was a learned man who lived in a temple. He had been the advisor to the emperor (well, he was until the emperor became mad with power). Who was he? Was he a witch? A magician? He was neither. He was a guide. A guardian who had been entrusted with the custody of traditional and spiritual knowledge. A mentor to the people. People came from far and wide to see him. He was conventional in his methods, and people seemed to like that—at least they knew what to expect. They enjoyed his traditional ways of teaching; his orthodox rituals and ceremonies unquestionably had been passed down from generation to generation. Altering them was preposterous; there was no need to rock the boat. He was very calm and there was a glow that seemed to ooze out of his every pore. They all came before him, as bees to flowers. At night, he would be found standing on a pedestal of books, the moon shining bright behind him, illuminating him in a radiance. He was the source of all knowledge; he had absorbed it all, from many centuries of teachings. His words delved deep into the soul, and no one argued. They followed him blindly, taking in every word he said, and absorbed it into their own soul. His teachings, traditional and conventional as they may be, provided the people with the structure they required and felt they needed. He knew his responsibilities and was careful to ensure he set an example. I mean, if he did not practice what he was teaching, then his congregation would never follow his example. So, they trusted him—he was the bridge between heaven and earth and their mentor to eternal peace.

MEANING

This card is about traditional institutions and may involve religious figures or mentors. The card asks you to question where the beliefs you hold have come from. Are they yours or have you been "taught" them? You are perhaps thinking of joining some sort of structured learning class or leaving a learning that no longer aligns with your beliefs or values anymore. You may come across someone who may end up being a mentor or a guide to you; listen to what they have to say, but keep an open mind and take only what resonates with you. You do not have to believe everything you are told. Make sure you are taking responsibility for your own beliefs and not surrendering them to another.

PERSON

The Mentor person is someone who is quite grounded in their spiritual beliefs and convictions. They can be very supportive and almost come across as a guide. They know who they are, and it can be extremely difficult to sway them from what they believe in. They will be quite stubborn and defend their beliefs to the end. They can be quite traditional and conventional and appear to be set in their ways. You can depend on them to be reliable and steady. They are quite conservative, and you know what you are going to get with them on a day-to-day basis. They tend not to stray too far from the norm. They need to be careful of becoming too fanatical and imposing their way and beliefs onto everyone else, and as such be seen as a fundamentalist.

THOUGHTS

Have you ever considered where the beliefs you hold have come from? What are the main beliefs you hold, and are they really yours or what you have been told to believe in? Consider creating new traditions or rituals for yourself or your family (or both). What would they be?

Desire, relationships, choice, passion, union, romance

VI
The Lovers

Every heart sings a song, incomplete, until another heart whispers back. Those who wish to sing always find a song. At the touch of a lover, everyone becomes a poet.

—Plato

KEYWORDS

Desire, relationships, choice, passion, union, romance

Once upon a time there was an ice queen. Her heart had been frozen for years, and nobody could thaw it. That was until she saw him. He was fire. His golden hair, piercing eyes, and gentle demeanor instilled a sense of warmth in her. He knew as soon as he saw her that she was different. He saw through her icy blonde hair and snowy-white skin, straight into her heart. He grabbed her by the waist and there was a loud **CRACK**. Her heart was starting to melt; the sheer touch of this mysterious stranger was enough for the ice to thaw. After all these years of guarding her heart, embracing the cold, and protecting herself, she was completely and utterly destroyed at the hands of the flames the stranger's love brought. They circled up into the night sky, her blonde hair sparkling in the moonlight, their eyes fixated on nothing but each other. They were ready to do anything for each other: their gaze was intense and passionate, and they were holding on to each other and never planning to let go. Was this the beginning of something?

MEANING

This card is all about a partnership, whether it is love or business. It is about expressing what you feel and making sure you make a balanced decision. This can also be about having to make a choice regarding important relationships (not necessarily love). We may be looking at them through "rose-tinted" glasses and even putting them on a pedestal, when in reality they are just as human as you and me, with all their flaws and imperfections. Are you looking for some great love to come and rescue you from a situation you may find yourself in? This card can remind us that there is no greater love than self-love. We do not need a knight in shining armor to complete us. We can be whole if we learn to love and value our self. For some, there may be a choice between two lovers!

PERSON

The Lovers person is all about relationships and romance! This is a person who makes choices from the heart. They feel most comfortable when they are around people and especially love being part of a couple, where they give their all. They are very good at balancing their emotions and tend to be full of life and love for the world and themselves. They see beauty in everything and gain much joy from forming new relationships—not necessarily romantic. They are honest and have an open heart, and they allow themselves to be vulnerable. After all, what is life without love? Some Lovers people are desperately needing love and approval since they do not have the capacity to love themselves. They can sometimes have issues with commitment, since they spend a lot of time in and out of various relationships, enjoying the initial adrenaline rush.

THOUGHTS

Do you have difficulty truly loving yourself? Why? Take someone whom you do not get along with, and look at them through the love of your inner spirit. Can you see why they are the way they are?

Victory, success, willpower, control, forward movement, force, ambition

VII
The Chariot

Whenever you want to achieve something, keep your eyes open, concentrate, and make sure you know exactly what it is you want. No one can hit their target with their eyes closed.

—Paulo Coelho

KEYWORDS

Victory, success, willpower, control, forward movement, force, ambition

Once upon a time there was a charioteer who traveled both the land and air in her chariot powered by two horses. In fact, she loved traveling and being in control of where she was heading. At least this way, if she made a mistake, she could not blame anyone else. Through her spyglass she looked down onto the world below. She saw love, friendship, money, and power, and she wanted it too. She knew that she could have it all. She just needed to learn to control the thoughts in her head that told her she couldn't achieve her desires. Her two horses, her constant companions, had a habit of playing up at times, each trying to control her, especially when she was on a mission. In fact, right now, she could see her destination through the spyglass—she knew where she wanted to head to—yet the dark horse started to gallop in the opposite direction, putting her off balance. "STOP!" she yelled. He was always trying to push ahead, always trying to take her in the opposite direction of where she wanted to go. He was like a stubborn child! The horse stopped, and she turned her attention to the second horse. He was as white as snow; it was almost pure. The woman was mesmerized by this magnificent creature: he had a gentle aura surrounding him. He made the woman feel calm and collected; he made her think. He represented the small amount of control the woman had left inside her. The woman's grip on the dark horse loosened as she made her way toward the white creature, bound them both together, and took hold of the reins. She sat back down, confident in the knowledge that the white horse was stronger and would be able to control the dark one. She picked up her spyglass and took another look at the world down below. It was time she was confident in her abilities to take charge of the animals and head victoriously toward her destiny.

MEANING

This card is all about triumph and having achieved what you desired through sheer willpower and control. The Chariot is about confidence in your abilities in being focused and disciplined in achieving your goals. It's very easy to be pulled away by distractions, but true victory comes when we remove the distractions from our path and focus on what it is we need, and pursue what we desire—no matter what the obstacle!

PERSON

The Chariot person is someone who is constantly on the move. They do not like staying in the same place for long, and if for any reason they have to, it can send them into anxiety. They are very strong-willed characters and determined to succeed. Nothing can stand in their way. They do not give up, and as long as they are willing to put in the effort and show discipline and control, there is no reason for them not to achieve what they desire. They do need to learn to listen to other people's needs and feelings before charging ahead, to ensure everyone is heading in the same direction; otherwise they run the risk of coming across as arrogant and domineering. The Chariot person may act confident, but underneath it all there may hide a quite vulnerable person, which many do not get to see, and it may take a while for others to break through the Chariot person's defenses to reach the soft core hidden away from the world.

THOUGHTS

What does success mean to you? What are your strategies for maintaining focus and control when there is chaos around you?

VIII Strength

You gain strength, courage, and confidence by every experience in which you really stop to look fear in the face.

—Eleanor Roosevelt

KEYWORDS

Bravery, patience, pride, determination, courage, endurance, compassion

Once upon a time there was a wee hummingbird who loved to travel. One night as he flew through a forest, he came across a fierce-looking dragon. The dragon lay along the forest floor, his eyes a fiery yellow glow. He was a feared creature. Nobody dared to stand up to him, since no one had lived to do so. The dragon was not always like this; he had been a good creature, friend to all. But the power he held over others had gone to his head and earned him a reputation as a terrifying monster. No one ever came near him anymore. They were too scared. The hummingbird was terrified and wanted to fly away, yet something stopped him. He knew that just because he was tiny in comparison to the dragon, it did not mean he was any less powerful. He flew right up to the dragon, staring him dead in the eye. The dragon was shocked. No creature had ever had the guts to come near him. He stared at the calm little bird with his ferocious yellow eyes, hoping to scare him away. The hummingbird may have been small, but a brave soul was he. He continued to hover beside the dragon, completely unafraid. "Interesting," the hummingbird thought to himself and flew closer. The dragon sat still, staring at the bird. As the sun crept up behind the trees, the bird came even closer and sat on the tip of the dragon's nose. He could see how beautiful the dragon was, and gazed tenderly into his eyes. The dragon's eyes softened, and all his fierceness vanished at that moment. He smiled as he heard a voice whisper to him, "You're not really as scary as you think." They were now forever connected.

MEANING

In life—like the hummingbird in the story above—we all at some point(s) have fears to face. They can be real-life dangers or even our inner demons. This card is about having the inner strength to stand up to whatever comes your way. Sometimes what we fear is not real, and its constructs we have created in our mind. Never think that you are too small or not enough to overcome whatever challenges come your way. You DO have courage, strength, patience, and determination to keep going.

PERSON

The Strength person is someone who has strong willpower, is confident, and shows great leadership. They have a tremendous amount of inner strength, with a strong lust for life, and are not afraid to go where others dare not. They are compassionate and caring and make great friends because they love to listen and offer advice. They have hearts of gold and would give you the shirt off their back if you needed it. They face their fears head on with courage and confidence. They may come across as bold and brave on the outside, but sometimes—underneath all that—there lies a person who allows themselves to give into their fears, rendering them scared and with low self-esteem. A far cry from the confident image they like to portray.

THOUGHTS

What are some of the things that scare you? Do you know why? What risks are you willing to take to try something that you fear doing?

IX
The Hermit

There is a wilderness we walk alone. However well-companioned . . .
—Stephen Vincent Benét

KEYWORDS

Loneliness, solitude, inspiration, introspection, stillness, contemplation, meditation

Once upon a time there was a woman who needed some time alone. She had a lot on her mind, and the world was way too chaotic for her to think straight. She ended up perched on top of a strange stone building, in the middle of the ocean. It was a foggy night and the sea was misty. She could not see ahead of her, but she knew there was a way in somewhere among the mist. It was how her mind had been recently—foggy—and she had been unable to see a way out. The middle of the ocean was far away from everyone. Just perfect. She watched as the waves crashed around her. There was not another soul in sight—just her and her thoughts. The moon was shining even brighter than usual as she sat there. The stars hung above her, as if dangling in the air by invisible strings. How did she get there? Even she didn't know. All she knew was that she was on her own, and she loved it. To many, solitude is a dark place, but not to her. She hated the hustle and bustle of the city, the constant noise of voices around her. She liked nothing more than to sit with her own thoughts. She had often found herself in this spot, when she wanted to listen to what her soul whispered. She would sit for hours, with not a person in sight. It was just her, the stars, and the moon. Sometimes she had the birds to keep her company, which she didn't mind; they usually minded their own business and left her to hers. She had been lost in the fog for a long time, not knowing what she had to do. As she sat atop her perch, watching the swirling fog dance around her, it suddenly cleared. She could see the way ahead. A clock floated on by, its ticktock distracting her momentarily. Time was passing, but she was in no rush. She would stay a while longer, chatting to her soul, until she was ready to join the world again.

MEANING

This card indicates a time for soul searching and inner work. Perhaps something is bothering you, and you are not getting the space and time to think. There may be too many distractions. All the answers that you seek are within you, and you may need to remove yourself physically to a quiet place where you can hear yourself think. Taking yourself away from a chaotic situation may allow you to listen to the voice within you that is crying out to be heard. This card can also indicate someone who is spending TOO much time alone and maybe has forgotten how to rejoin the world again. If you are on your own too often, consider why that is. Are you hiding from something or someone?

PERSON

The Hermit person is someone who tends to live a solitary life, keeping to themselves. They enjoy time spent in solitude, quietly observing what goes on around them. They do not feel the need to impress anyone, preferring to live on their own, on their terms. Because they spend so much time alone, they have great knowledge from books, they can be great advisors for those who seek wisdom. They like to help people and can be a great laugh, but after a while of socializing they long to get back to their solitude. They tend to have very few close friends, because of which not everyone understands them. Not that it bothers them. In some cases, the Hermit person may be someone who is very lonely, and although they have chosen to isolate, it may be because they no longer know how to function in the world.

THOUGHTS

How often do you allow yourself to retreat from the hustle and bustle of daily life? Do you find yourself on your own a lot of the time? Why is that?

Fortune, luck, destiny, karma, fate, opportunity, randomness, change

X
The Wheel of Destiny

Let us follow our destiny, ebb and flow. Whatever may happen, we master fortune by accepting it.

—Virgil

KEYWORDS

Fortune, luck, destiny, karma, fate, opportunity, randomness, change

Once upon a time, high in the cosmos, there turned a great golden wheel of destiny. The wheel was in constant motion, symbolizing the continuity of all human existence being in the constant flux of change that was encountered in daily lives. Here upon this wheel of destiny was where the Three Sisters of Fate would meet. These goddesses presided over the sacred laws of life and shared a bond of connectivity as they wove the tapestry of life, which doled out the fate of what each mortal would experience in their lifetime.

Each one of these sisters had her own responsibilities—a maiden who was responsible for which soul would be born and when they would incarnate. She would spin out strands of DNA dressed in green, signifying new life, freshness, and growth. The second sister, wearing blue, wanted to show that years of experience is actually the best part of life to be celebrated. She was the matron, and she imprinted her symbol of the horoscope upon the great wheel, displaying the importance of the in-between, that sweet space between Life and Death. She wanted to remind mortals that it is not when you were born or how you will die; it is how you lived your life that counted. She would intertwine the strands of other life souls, determining how long the souls spent with one another. The third sister, holding a pair of shears, in her crone years had been entrusted to cut the thread by ending a mortal's life. She wore a crimson robe symbolizing the blood that must be shed, for without death there could be no life anew. She was revered and honored as the taker of life, a task that weighed down heavily on her shoulders, because with the celebration of any new birth came the whispered promise of death. Floating to the side of the wheel was the hovering hand, representing awareness.

MEANING

Sometimes people cannot see beyond the hand, and that prevents them from uncovering the deeper mysteries of the three fates. The hand that spins the wheel symbolizes the thought process of the mundane, where we humans think we are the ones in control, and when we feel that we have lost control, we blame that same hand on chance and bad luck, coincidences. We believe in the old adage that "round and round she goes, and where she stops nobody knows." The Wheel of Destiny is here to remind you that by exercising free will you can have a life of your design and follow your creative and intuitive pursuits to fulfillment, but also if you simply cast your gaze just beyond the hand you will see the Goddesses of Fate that always have a hand in your birth, significant karmic events, and your death.

PERSON

The Wheel of Destiny person is someone who is always on the move, searching for new changes and new perspectives in life. They are seen as someone who is very lucky and somehow just happens to be in the right place at the right time. They tend to live life and never lose their center, no matter what is going on with them, trusting in the universe. Some Wheel of Destiny people may find themselves in cycles of abundance and scarcity, where their lack of organization and planning may lead to them being unprepared when their lives are in a downturn. However, these people are so lucky that no matter what, due to pure chance, an opportunity will come their way and they will land on their feet.

THOUGHTS

Think about the times when things have not worked out for you, or you have felt as if fate had dealt you a "bad hand." Looking back with hindsight, can you now see what was going on behind the scenes?

Justice, balance, fairness, impartiality, legal matters, wisdom

XI
Justice

Injustice anywhere is a threat to justice everywhere.
—Martin Luther King Jr.

KEYWORDS

Justice, balance, fairness, impartiality, legal matters, wisdom

Once upon a time there was a blind woman dressed in green robes who hid her eyes behind dark glasses. In her hand, she carried the Sword of Truth and the Scales of Balance. She was a beacon of light in an unfair world, and people came from far and wide to express their situation, in the hope that she would deliver the justice she was famed for. She was known to deliver her verdicts on the basis of the facts presented to her, considering and balancing all evidence and deliberating long and hard to ensure the final conclusion was fair. She was Truth and Integrity. She rarely showed any emotions, which she knew came in the way of making a rational, fair, and balanced decision. She had seen it often enough, people getting all emotional and making the wrong decisions, which they usually regretted. Decisions made out of anger, fear, love, etc. It was why they then came to her—to discern the truth from the emotions surrounding it. She often stood alone, surrounded by her prized red roses. It was a softer side of her that not many people knew. That part was private to her, never interfering in her path, never letting emotion cloud her ability to make a judgment, and that was the key to her success. This was rare in a world where emotions prevail over most things, and this is why people trusted her more than anything else. People knew that when they came to her, they would get the truth, the whole truth, and nothing but the truth!

MEANING

The Justice card is about laws—whether they be human or universal laws. It's about making decisions from the head rather than the heart. Be rational. Be calm and deal with it logically. There may be a legal aspect coming up or currently ongoing—a divorce, legal case, etc. This card can indicate that this legal matter will be resolved in a fair and just manner. If it is you who has been doing something illegal, then there is a chance the result will not be in your favor. Justice asks you to be aware of the law that states actions have consequences, so if you have been the one hurting someone, then it's about time you take responsibility for your actions, or you may just get what you deserve! Consequently, if you have been on the receiving end of someone's negative intent, then be aware that justice will be served.

PERSON

The Justice person is someone who is fair, balanced, and just. They are honest individuals who have no time for lies and will stand up for injustice. They have very strong moral ethics and will defend their principles with vigor. They have a strong sense of right and wrong and often take their time arriving at a decision. When they do have a decision to make, they will carefully consider all the evidence available with an objective eye. Emotions or feelings will not play a part in whatever decision they arrive at. Only the cold, hard facts. As friends, they will tell you as it is—no sugar coating—so if you are looking for an honest opinion, then they are not the people to go to, unless you can stomach the harsh reality they will deliver.

THOUGHTS

How often do YOU accept responsibility when things go wrong for you? Think of a situation or situations where you blamed someone else, when actually it was as a result of actions YOU took.

XII
Perspective

Patience is power. Patience is not an absence of action; rather it is "timing." It waits on the right time to act, for the right principles, and in the right way.

—Fulton J. Sheen

KEYWORDS

Perspective, limbo, sacrifice, letting go, surrender, enlightenment, delays, reflection, insight

Once upon a time there was a person who had it all, yet she still felt as if she was stuck in a rut. Most days she ran through the forest. She encountered the same familiar animals she had seen hundreds of times before. This was her daily ritual, and she had done so since she was a little girl. She ran past the familiar oak tree and the familiar river and jumped over the familiar fallen tree trunk. She had memorized this route like the back of her hand. As she approached the familiar opening where she would sit and read, she had a thought. Maybe it was time for a change? She had known nothing but these familiar woods for many years; nothing much had changed. Maybe some new flowers, a few more animals, but everything was pretty much the same. She climbed up the tree she would usually sit under and walked across one of the tree's thick branches. She sat down and hung upside down. The forest looked so different. Although everything was upside down, it was a welcome change to what she had always known. She hung for a while, taking in her new surroundings. The forest was still the same, yet somehow she was different now. It was as if hanging upside down had given her a whole new perspective of the place. She still ran through the forest every day, but now she took her time and looked at the things she had missed over the years she had been walking here. It was as if she had been reborn.

MEANING

Right before something new begins and something old has died, there is a time of nothingness. When time just seems to stand still. This is the card of Perspective. It is a time to surrender and be still. The time to act is not now. This is a time to be still and observe what is going on around you. With this card, you may feel as if you are "waiting in limbo." Again, patience is advised. There is nothing you can do at this moment in time but to just remain still and spend time in reflection, until the next step reveals itself. The card urges you to spend time alone and decide what you are willing to lose in order to move forward, since until then you will remain where you are.

PERSON

The Perspective person is an unconventional individual who can be quite creative and forward thinking. They recognize the importance of taking their time to look at all sides of a situation. They do not rush into things, and instead wait and watch, biding their time, before they act. They may even sacrifice elements of themselves for the higher good or cause. They can be daydreamers, living in their own ideas and beliefs. They may find their dreams are quite vivid, and they may even live in them as an escape from daily life. Perspective people may be found outdoors and in nature activities, which seems to allow them to escape into a whole new magical world.

THOUGHTS

Think of a situation where you have felt "stuck." Did you need to make a sacrifice of something or someone to overcome the feeling of "stuckness"? Maybe you are in such a dilemma now. What are you willing or unwilling to let go of, in order to begin moving again?

Endings, beginnings, transition, transformation, regeneration, renewal, rebirth

XIII
Death

What is dead may never die, but rises again harder and stronger.
—The Greyjoys (*Game of Thrones*)

KEYWORDS

Endings, beginnings, transition, transformation, regeneration, renewal, rebirth

Once upon a time there was a woman whose world had been dark for too long. Death had taken away her most precious person. She would visit the grave daily, as she had done since she was small. One day, as she approached, she noticed the silhouette of a little girl standing at the foot of the grave. "Who are you?" the woman asked. The little girl didn't respond. She stared blankly at the ground, with a pendant clock in her hand. The woman recognized the familiar red curls of the girl's hair. They looked exactly like her hair did when she was a little girl. Staring intently, she noticed that the girl's face bore a similar resemblance to her: Could it be? The little girl was she. The woman stared at the blank look on the girl's face, a face that had never changed throughout the years. Death had taken its toll on the girl for too long; she had missed out on a normal childhood out of fear of letting go. Even now in her womanhood, she bore the same look on her face. Enough was enough. It was time to let go. "I need to let go," the woman thought. The little girl looked up for the first time, a smile forming on her lips. The flower the woman was holding started to glow. Was it the light finally coming back into her life? Color began to appear on the woman, and her fiery red hair was once again noticeable. Greenery started to surround the gravestone, and the ghostly figure of the woman's past started to fade. The woman understood that with death comes a chance for rebirth. This was her chance at a new life: one of change, joy, and beauty, which was possible only once she had been able to let go of her past.

MEANING

The Death card is a card of transformation, of metamorphosis. A phase of your life is coming to an end, and there is nothing that you can do to stop it. Just as death is final, this change will not be reversible, and nothing will be the same again. It's time to put the past behind you and move on stronger and transformed. Do not fight it or try to resist it, since this change is coming whether you like it or not, and resisting it will only cause you pain. Sometimes we hold on to things because it would be painful to let go, but if we do not let go of the old, how then will we welcome the new that is waiting in the wings to come to us?

PERSON

The Death person is someone who comes across as mysterious, secretive, and intense, who have undergone huge transformations in life. They do not avoid change, nor do they fear it, as they can handle anything life throws at them, seeing them as opportunities for growth. These people nearly always experience very strong and intense emotions. Their task in this lifetime is to learn to master them, because if they don't, then their inner life will be very difficult. Death card people have learned how to use their intense emotions to motivate them to change and grow. Some of these people may struggle with holding on to the past, accepting it, and letting it go. This then keeps them stuck and stops them from growing as individuals and moving forward. They need to learn that there is strength in surrender, and can move on to another phase in life only once they have let the old go.

THOUGHTS

In what ways are you resisting changes to your life? Is there something you need to let go of, that no longer serves you?

Balance, harmony, calm, serenity, peace, healing, diplomacy, moderation

XIV
Temperance

Problems arise in that one has to find a balance between what people need from you and what you need for yourself.

—Jessye Norman

KEYWORDS

Balance, harmony, calm, serenity, peace, healing, diplomacy, moderation

Once upon a time, a woman dressed in yellow took a walk through the woods. She thought about all the responsibilities that she had in her life and how unbalanced she felt. Surely, there had to be a way to balance all she had on her plate. She walked deeper into the forest, the light fading away with every step she took. Suddenly, she came to a single streetlight hidden away by the vast greenery. The light was dim but just bright enough for her to make out two feathers lying on the ground in front of her. One was dark and frayed and looked old; one was white like the snow and was pure and intact. As she looked at the feathers, she realized that they symbolized her predicament. The black feather represented one extreme existence of life (the parties, the emotions, the unhealthy diet, etc.), while the white feather represented another extreme (obsessive dieting, hermit-like existence, etc.). Life seemed to swing like a pendulum for her. At times it was all black, and at other times VERY white. At that moment, she realized that it was very rarely "in between" or "gray." She had spent too long living life in excessive extremes, and this is what was upsetting her inner harmony. If she could blend the two and live a life of prudence and moderation, then she would be able to live a truly balanced life. Realistically, she knew that it would be very hard to maintain a constant "gray" life, but as she looked at the feather, she understood that it was okay to sometimes swing to the black or white, as long as she came back to her center.

MEANING

This card looks at how much in balance we are. It is about being moderate, in all aspects of life. Want that chocolate cake? Go ahead and have a piece of it, just not all of it! Yes, we can sometimes allow ourselves to go to extremes, as long as we come back to our center. This card suggests that if things have been out of balance, then this is a good time to assess where we are out of equilibrium and to bring life back into harmony. If you are feeling out of sync, then stop and tune in to your body. What is it trying to tell you? Do you have a good work-life balance or is the pendulum swinging too much in one direction, and at what cost? What can you do to bring yourself back into alignment.

PERSON

The Temperance person is someone who strives to maintain balance in all aspects of their life. They tend to live quite a moderate lifestyle, hardly venturing to extremes. They make great friends and good listeners, since they do not take sides and will listen to both sides before dishing out advice. They are not afraid to compromise and will do so, if it means keeping the peace. Whether that be mental, emotional, physical, or spiritual, maintaining equilibrium between these aspects is important to them. They are happy to just sit still and chill, taking in their surroundings. They are quite peaceful people and get along well with others—not being too emotional or too detached. They can be quite creative people who are not afraid to try something new, even mixing new techniques with the old, creating their own blend of "something." They can be found as teachers, artists, musicians, chefs, or anything that requires creativity, and they love traveling, since it broadens their horizons. Because they prefer a nice, quiet life, they can be manipulated by others, where they end up compromising more that they should.

THOUGHTS

Take an honest look at places where you overindulge or underindulge. What effect does that have on your life?

Obsession, control, domination, addiction, temptation, materialism, ambition

XV
The Devil

Fear is the dark room where the Devil develops his negatives.
—Gary Busey

KEYWORDS

Obsession, control, domination, addiction, temptation, materialism, ambition

Once upon a time, a woman lived in a dark underground room. Her job was to make people feel trapped and restricted. Her eyes were a fiery yellow, and there was something extremely sinister about them. People always fell for her special look of gentle concern, when all along she was looking at them with pity and contempt. When outside forces were beyond the control of ordinary men, she was there. She was the creature that parents warned their children about in order to prevent them from turning to the temptations of alcohol, greed, and anger. The bars that surrounded her were there to keep the temptations out, but they were not very strong; in fact, they were almost transparent. The material objects, the greed, and the anger had become too much for some people, and those were her favorite kind of people. Where she took them, nobody knew. Down into the deepest depths of the psyche was where she stayed, chains and cages littered all around her. These cages were usually full of people who had strayed too far. She did not even have to lock the cages; they were too controlled and addicted by their desires to see that they could leave at any time. She emphasized people's worst qualities and drew out the bad. She stared from behind the bars with her fiery eyes, the cracks in her skin glowing like molten lava. She was their worst fear. Could she curb their temptations? Or did she signify the end? Oh how she loved playing with these people. They were her puppets, and she their master.

MEANING

The Devil is the card of control, manipulation, and deception, signifying a part of your life where you are feeling trapped, almost like you cannot escape and are stuck. It is about temptation and addiction. We can be addicted to something that we think is good for us, and give our power away to that very thing, allowing ourselves to be controlled by it. What we don't realize is that we have the power to break free from the addiction, but because it's easier to blame someone else for our predicament, we end up in the situation, not realizing that escape is in our own hands. This card may also indicate a dependency on drugs or some other substance. There may even be a person who has taken control of your life, where there may even be abuse (physical, mental, or emotional), yet you feel bound to them—you might have been in a toxic situation for so long that you have forgotten there's a way out. You DO have the power to break free.

PERSON

The Devil person is an individual who is charming, charismatic, and highly ambitious. They come across as quite intense and, at times, obsessive and have the ability to be highly focused on a task until it is complete. They can get things done where others give up. Nothing is taboo for these people. They are quite persistent and practical and make great business people, due to their entrepreneurial abilities. They may love power, the more the better, and love to surround themselves with equally important people. Devil people may find themselves easily prone to addictions—whether it's power, control, sex, money, or substances—as a means to cope with life. They can fall into victimhood mode, blaming factors outside of themselves, such as addictions, instead of looking at themselves and their part to play. Devil people love power, and they possess a very strong will, which if not kept in check can have them come across as controlling and domineering, using others, sometimes just for their own pleasure.

THOUGHTS

Whom or what have you allowed to enslave you? List areas in your life where this is the case, and look at what was going on for you at the time.

XVI The Tower

Together, they would watch everything that was so carefully planned collapse, and they would smile at the beauty of destruction.
—Markus Zusak

KEYWORDS

Upheaval, disgrace, calamity, release, downfall, flash of insight, revelation

Once upon a time there was a man who lived life according to his beliefs and ways. He had been ignoring signs from the universe to change certain elements of his life. His attitude had been to brush it under the carpet; he would worry about it later. He didn't think anything of it. "What was the worst that could happen?" he would think. Life was about living in the moment, so what if there were troubling signs along the way—it would work out, wouldn't it? Year after year of continuing as he was had begun to take a toll on him. One day, out of the blue, he felt a sudden fire raging in his head, the flames swirling around looking for a way out into the air. He had finally arrived at a breaking point. There was no space left within him to contain his outdated beliefs and the lies he had told himself. He had been struck by the lightning of truth, and everything was going to come down to this one moment when everything would burst from him and he would explode. The walls of ignorance and bliss he had built over the years suddenly exploded and shattered before his eyes. The fire was fierce and destroyed everything in its path. All that remained was a pile of charred rubble. His world had been turned upside down. Sifting through the still-smoldering rubble, he looked at what remained. The routines he had created, the stability that he thought he would always have, had ceased to exist. He knew that it was time to create something more stable, to rebuild his life from the rubble that lay below him. He would begin anew.

MEANING

When the Tower appears, it can indicate a sudden shift or a sudden change or an upcoming calamity or upheaval. The Tower card heralds shock or a chaotic situation that came out of the blue and completely destroyed everything you have ever believed in. It may be that the signs were there all along and you ignored them, until it culminated in the disaster in front of you now. The Tower card, although it causes destruction of the old ways and beliefs, allows you the chance to rebuild something new and stronger in its place. It can signify that the things you thought were real were an illusion constructed by the mind, to keep you in a certain situation. This card can indicate that you're experiencing a spiritual awakening from which you will emerge as a wiser, stronger person. The Tower forces you to examine which areas of your life are based on lies and which ones are the real thing.

PERSON

The Tower person is someone with immense strength and fortitude. They have the ability to withstand whatever storm comes their way, and they understand that nothing in life is permanent. Everything eventually changes, no matter how permanent it may seem. Some of them have the ability to cope with change, while others may need a sudden shock to the system, forcing them to change their ways. They may have faced much chaos in their lifetime, and every storm has left a mark on their personality, making them who they are today. They may also come across as argumentative, and they love upsetting the status quo, rocking the very foundations of institutions or ways of thinking that have existed forever, just for the sake of it. They can be activists, who want to tear down the old ways, ushering in a new era. Trouble may follow them where they go, and their relationships may have lots of drama as a result of their volatile, unstable nature, which may include anger issues, tantrums, and meltdowns.

THOUGHTS

Is there a situation in your life where a drastic change is required? If so, what is preventing you from making the changes?

Renewal, hope, inspiration, serenity, calm, wishes, dreams, healing, miracles

Though my soul may set in darkness, it will rise in perfect light; I have loved the stars too fondly to be fearful of the night.

—Sarah Williams

KEYWORDS

Renewal, hope, inspiration, serenity, calm, wishes, dreams, healing, miracles

Once upon a time there was a star. She had watched the world as it entered a period of destruction, which destroyed everything in its path. When she returned to assess the damage caused by the wave of darkness, she saw that things were calmer now. The stars were twinkling brighter than usual to signify the light at the end of the tunnel, lighting up the darkness of the desolate wasteland. The universal clock that was once invisible due to the dark was now in full view. She wanted to fast-forward time to make it seem like nothing had happened, but she knew that through destruction came light. The clock had been stuck like that for a while, and she wanted to get it going again. The darkness had hidden the keys to the mechanics, and the woman was determined to get it moving again; she was determined that it was time for the light to shine. She just had to find the key to start it. Under her hat, she stored a bunch of keys, and she took them out. One by one she tried each key in a lock, and soon enough the cogs were ignited with a golden light. The clock that had stood still was moving and the mechanics were turning. She had done it. As light radiated from the cogs and the stars twinkled, she realized that light had once again been restored to the world, and the darkness that was once prevalent had been diminished for now. The wait had all been worth it, for she knew that should the darkness reappear, it would only be a matter of time before her trusty keys would once again let the light shine and get the world turning again.

MEANING

The Star card is a beacon of light after the darkness. A symbol of guidance and hope. A card of peace, calmness, and inspiration. It asks us to focus on what lies ahead in the future, rather than looking back. You have come through whatever hardships befell you in the past, and now is the time to embrace all the amazing possibilities life has in store for you. You will regain what you lost; just have faith in the universe. It's your time now to shine big and bright. Be the light that goes out into the world, illuminating the dark places where hope does not exist. Shine your light into the darkness and allow hope and faith to take bloom. If you are wishing for something, then the Star asks you to have faith in yourself and what you desire. I tend to see this card as the card of wishes coming true. But only if you keep the faith and do not lose hope!

PERSON

The Star person is the eternal optimist, full of hope, idealism, and inspiration. They are humanitarians and philosophers, idealistic and artistic in nature. They believe that no matter how dark the night, as long as there is even a speck of hope, then there will be a brighter dawn. Highly compassionate, they use it to serve humanity and can often be found shining their light and bringing hope in the darkest reaches of the world, where hope is a word that has long been forsaken. They are honest, truthful people who have a clear direction of where they are heading in life. The can see the bigger picture, which makes them a wise friend to have when you are mired in details. The Star person may be endowed with highly creative gifts such as music, art, writing, or poetry, which they will endeavor to share with the world, doing their little bit in making it a better place, full of peace and beauty. They can be too idealistic at times, not seeing situations or people as they are, but as they want them to be, and this can lead to disappointment at times.

THOUGHTS

Spend time in the quiet contemplating your hopes, aspirations, dreams, and goals. Dream about where you would like to see yourself in the next five years. What will it look like?

Mystery, subconscious, secrecy, illusion, fear, phobias, paranoia, obsession

XVIII
The Moon

The moon will guide you through the night with her brightness, but she will always dwell in the darkness, in order to be seen.
—Shannon L. Alder

KEYWORDS

Mystery, subconscious, secrecy, illusion, fear, phobias, paranoia, obsession

Once upon a time there was a woman who lived by the sea. Time after time, she had stood at the shoreline and stared out at the vast body of water that lay before her. She had never ventured out there for fear of the unknown. Who knew what kinds of creatures and monsters were lurking in the dark waters? It was always so dark, and she knew better than to go exploring in a place she feared. Many times she thought about facing her fear and seeing what lay beyond the area she had known. But then again, maybe it was safer for her to stay put. She could just about make out the monstrous creatures that lived on the water. No way was she going out there! One night the moon was especially bright, and the woman saw that she could now see the water quite clearly. It glistened in the moonlight, almost sparkling. It was a magical sight. It looked inviting, calming, and welcoming. She was in its spell. She hesitated no longer and walked straight toward it. As she walked, she saw a number of funny little creatures. They were unlike any she had seen before. They were small, almost half her size. Some had wings, some had fangs, but they were cute and funny, she thought. There was nothing scary about them. The farther she walked, the brighter the moon shone, and she could see she was now standing in the middle of the body of water she had been so scared to approach. There was nothing but bright-blue light and magic around her. Everything around her was illuminated by the moonlight, and it all seemed brighter. What she did not realize was that the moon illuminated only part of the ocean. Under the sea, it was still dark, and who knows what creatures lived there. It was a false sense of security. She reached out and took hold of the moon, thinking that she had found her guiding light. She did not know that it was all too easy to lose her way in the moonlight, since it could be deceptive. She was stuck in her illusion, thinking the moon had revealed all the secrets of the dark to her, when in actual fact it was showing her what she wanted to see. She was well and truly caught up in the magical realm of fantasy.

MEANING

The Moon card represents deception, illusions, lies, underhanded behavior, and the unknown. You may be feeling more emotional than usual at this time. It can signify that there is more underneath the surface than you're aware of. This card can also ask us to "tread carefully," since in the moonlight, things are not what they seem, with the moon revealing hidden desires, worries, fears, and phobias that lie in our most secretive depths, distorting our vision. The Moon card can also signify a period of heightened emotions that may lead to confusion. It may be linked to hidden memories of past times, buried issues, or repressions surfacing now, leaving you feeling vulnerable and confused.

PERSON

The Moon person is someone who is extremely intuitive, receptive, and highly empathetic. They may come across as introverted and mysterious, keeping a part of them hidden away. They may be prone to mood swings, instability, and may sometimes have difficulty distinguishing between reality and fantasy. They can show great creativity, psychic powers, and visions and may exhibit sudden intuitive flashes that are accurate. Since this is the card of illusions, who you think this person is may not be who they actually are! They love trawling into the deepest part of the mind and can be found in careers related to the mind, such as psychology or investigators.

THOUGHTS

If you are feeling extra emotional at this time, consider some creative way in which you can express yourself.

XIX The Sun

Sunshine will guide your heart even on the most darkest of days.
—Anthony T. Hincks

KEYWORDS

Success, enlightenment, joy, happiness, child, optimism, innocence

Once upon a time there were a brother and sister. They had just moved to a new city and lived next to an old, derelict building. They missed their happy home with happy memories. As they walked through the corridors of the empty building, they heard fairground music. Immediately their faces lit up like the sun, and they ran toward the music. Swinging open the huge steel doors, they were greeted with the most extraordinary sight. In the middle of the courtyard stood the biggest carousel they had ever seen in their lives. Every color of the rainbow adorned the carousel; there were horses of each color. The carousel itself was very grand indeed, taking up most of the space in the floor. Flowers, trees, and exotic wildlife surrounded it—a song of color all around them. The sun was extremely bright that day, its brilliant orange light reflecting off the carousel and emitting a golden glow all around them. They had never felt such contentment or happiness before. Their minds were racing, their eyes widening, and their hearts beating. They stood there in disbelief, taking the sight in. The music grew louder and louder, furthering their excitement. They looked at one another with a sly smirk on their faces and ran as fast as their legs could carry them, straight toward the carousel, and jumped on the first horse they could see. They played for hours, going around and around. It brought them nothing but sheer joy and happiness. It was the perfect day in a perfect place, and they were glowing.

MEANING

The Sun card signifies HAPPINESS! Good fortune and good times are indicated with this card. It is a card of positivity and assures you that good times are on the way, if they are not already. Look for the joys and blessings in your life. This card can also be associated with children, either your own or others', or pregnancy, or even a message to get in touch with the inner child within you. Remember the fun you used to have as a child; remember how little things used to bring you joy—why did it stop? Try to capture the essence of that small child and bring it into everything you do, and you will find that things will not be a chore but a source of joy. This card may indicate a new successful job where you will shine and be appreciated, or even a promotion to a position of status.

PERSON

The Sun person is someone who is confident and playful and loves being the center of attention. They are very happy, positive people and exude a warm ray of energy when they enter a room. You will know when there is a Sun person in the room, since they will be radiating such energy that people will have no option but to gravitate toward them. They enjoy life to its fullest and will try something new, even if they do it only once. Always up for a challenge and an adventure, these people have many friends due to their good nature and cheerfulness. They are natural extroverts, full of fun, and they can be found surrounded by people. The Sun person is the eternal optimist, believing that things will always turn out okay. They love to create, and, of course, what they create is bigger and better than anything anyone else has ever done! The Sun person can, however, be prone to bouts of pessimism, and they can sometimes become childish if they do not get their own way.

THOUGHTS

Today, spend a day outdoors and look at the amazing, joyous, wondrous things around you. What blessings are you grateful for? What makes you completely and utterly happy?

Judgment, rebirth, awakening, resurrection, inner calling, transformation

XX
Judgment

Sometimes you have to kind of die inside in order to rise from your own ashes and believe in yourself and love yourself to become a new person.

—Gerard Way

KEYWORDS

Judgment, rebirth, awakening, resurrection, inner calling, transformation

Once upon a time there was a young woman. She had been through so many challenges in her life and was now tired. She had spent her life lurching from one crisis to another, almost sleepwalking through life. She had alienated many people close to her, and they no longer cared about her. She had done this to herself. She realized that deceit, anger, and greed had consumed her and destroyed all those around her. Yet, still, she felt hope. She wandered the streets with her violin—her most prized possession—in her hand and then found a spot to rest. She sat down and drifted off into a deep sleep. There was a flash as a bolt of lightning struck the stones beside her. She woke with a start as she saw the ground smoking beside her. The smoke got heavier and suddenly flames appeared. The flames grew higher and higher until she could make out a figure emerging from the flames. The figure was tall and slim, dressed in white and holding a trumpet. They had a set of fiery wings and a stone-cold expression on their face. "Who are you?" the girl demanded. The voice was gentle. "I come to you to review your life and your actions. What do you have to say?" The girl looked at the figure, and suddenly her life flashed past her eyes. She saw it all—everything she had said, past misdeeds and kindnesses, her arrogance at thinking she was the best violinist in the world. She saw that the violin was a material possession that did not matter, since it would be left behind when she left this world. She could see clearly now how power, possessions, and status meant nothing. For one day, like others, she too was going to return to Spirit, where what you owned or what your status was would not matter. The only thing that would matter would be what you had done in this life, what you left behind as a legacy. She realized she had not been truly living before, but merely existing in a half-awake manner. She looked up at the figure and suddenly had a clarity of vision she had not had before. She knew what she had to do now. Her path was so very clear. She had been cleansed of the past and stood up with a purpose. Life was beckoning her.

MEANING

It may be time to be completely honest with yourself and look at where you are and how much of it is linked to decisions you have made or actions you have taken in the past. This is a card of rebirth, resurrection, and transformation in your life. You may be reevaluating your relationships, career, and your life at this time, not sure where they are going. It is a time to pay attention to any opportunities that may come up at this time, since you may find doors opening that will lead you to the next level.

PERSON

The Judgment person is someone who may have had to reinvent themselves due to a life-changing event or situation. They may have been living life in a routine manner and had a sudden shock that made them question what they were doing with their life and purpose. This may have resulted in them completely changing their life direction. They may change careers many times in their lifetime to realign with new understandings that may come to them during periods of transformation. They are great people to have around during a time of crisis, since they can help you see the way out.

THOUGHTS

Is there a situation in your past that you are still holding on to since it's too painful to face? Using a trusted friend or therapist, consider finding closure of the situation.

Completion, wholeness, attainment,
fulfillment, triumph, end of a cycle

XXI
The World

I feel like I'm on top of the world. Honestly, I feel like I've climbed a very giant mountain, and I'm just standing right on top with my arms wide open and breathing rarified air.

—Shania Twain

KEYWORDS

Completion, wholeness, attainment, fulfillment, triumph, end of a cycle

Once upon a time, during a full moon, a girl—young and naive—decided to go for a walk in the woods. Remember her? She was at the beginning of this journey, the one who went for a stroll and ended up entering a huge book. Yep, that same girl had been on a journey, and what a journey it had been, and what amazing people she had met along the way. Each and every one of those people had taught her something about herself, revealing parts of her that she did not know even existed. She had finally arrived at the end of the journey, and as she looked around, she could see the stars and the moon. She looked down and saw that in her hands was the world, wearing a huge gold crown. She could not believe it! She could actually see the woods that she had left in what seemed like a very long time ago. And look, there were the roses that had adorned the book that she had entered so long ago. They were shedding rose petals into space, just like the young girl had shed the many layers of herself along the way. The roses were hugging the world, reaching out to touch the crown in celebration of the young woman's success. She was now a woman, not the little naive girl who had started this journey. She now knew how to survive life, no matter what it put her through. She had all the ingredients needed within her. She was self-sufficient, and success was hers. As she basked in her accomplishment, she knew that the success she had achieved was not hers alone. It belonged to everyone else who had contributed to her growth, for they too had a part to play. For now, she was going to enjoy her time in the light, since she knew that she would not stop because there was more to strive for. This was only the beginning, and there were many more amazing adventures to be had.

MEANING

The World is a card of triumph, of success, and of having achieved what you wanted! Be very proud, since what you have accomplished may have involved a very long and arduous journey. But you did it! The World card signifies that it's time to acknowledge the hard work that got you where you are now. You may be feeling deeply satisfied with the results, and it is a time of joy and happiness. You may have come to the end of a journey, or you may have concluded a significant life cycle, and it's time for something new to begin again. The card can also indicate some sort of long-distance travel; if you are planning a trip, then it's a great time to do so, since it will be a very joyous trip indeed.

PERSON

The World person is an achiever, willing to give anything a try, giving them experience of many things. They live life by their own rules and own beliefs, and are quite independent, allowing them to be self-sufficient and responsible. They love to travel, and because of this they have a perspective that other people may not have. They may enjoy living away from home and exploring all that the world has to offer. Sometimes the World person may be plagued with feelings of insecurity and low self-worth, resulting in them running as far away as possible from difficult situations, rather than facing them.

THOUGHTS

How often do you allow yourself to delight in your accomplishments? Think of something you have recently achieved, and plan a celebration with friends. Be proud!

The Suit of Cups

Ace of Cups

The best and most-beautiful things in the world cannot be seen or even touched. They must be felt with the heart.

—Helen Keller

Something new, creation, potential, love, possibilities, overwhelming emotions

KEYWORDS

Something new, creation, potential, love, possibilities, overwhelming emotions

A hand emerges from the side of the image, a large cup balanced on its palm. The cup is made up of large metallic petals in blue, green, and purple hues. It looks as if the cup is being offered to the reader. The hand faces east, signifying things to come, which will have an effect in the future if the offer is accepted. Green ribbons are attached to the stem of the cup, which gently blow in the breeze. Large mountains are presented in the background, but they are not very clear, indicating that whatever the cup is offering is just the beginning of an emotional journey, which will culminate in something solid. Could it be a new love or a new stage within an existing relationship? The hearts flying into the cup certainly may indicate that. Whatever it is, the presence of the hearts shows that it will be something that you will completely fall in love with. The water flowing out of the cup seems to convey that whatever is being offered, you will love it so deeply that it could well you up and overwhelm you. The white dove flying toward the cup is a symbol of divine love, indicating that this gift or message has come from the universe. The moon shining down on the cup reflects our subconscious desires, signifying that perhaps this is something you have been desiring all along. Did you manifest this gift?

THOUGHTS

Have a think about something you were able to do, something that you pour your heart and soul into. What would it be? Is it time to maybe start doing just that?

Two of Cups

Soulmates, attraction, companionship, feelings, partnership, true love, affinity

Friendship—my definition—is built on two things. Respect and trust. Both elements have to be there. And it has to be mutual. You can have respect for someone, but if you don't have trust, the friendship will crumble.

—Steig Larsson

KEYWORDS

Soulmates, attraction, companionship, feelings, partnership, true love, affinity

Two flamingos, each decked in beautiful headgear, stand on one leg, with their beaks gently touching one another, indicating a meeting of the minds. Both have soft, shimmery wings. Behind them, a large doorway to a body of water stands, from which a lit chandelier is hung. Two cups are seen, one on each side of the entrance, with an arch of stardust flowing from one cup to the other. Each cup belongs to the individual flamingo, signifying a union of the two separate emotions into one. This is where the complementary energies of each of them are combining and undergoing a transformation. They each have their own separate gifts that they are bringing to this partnership, hoping to accomplish something that otherwise they might not have been able to do on their own. A large moon hovers over the water, casting a light. A seagull sits on one side of the entrance, its mouth open as if calling or announcing. The two flamingos do not seem to notice him, since they are so absorbed into each other. Is there something they need to be aware of? Are they so caught up in their love for one another that others are envious, and they cannot see the harm others wish to cause them? The seagull certainly does not look happy! Rose petals are strewn across the floor, like confetti, under the feet of the flamingos. It almost looks like a marriage is taking place. It may not be a literal marriage, but a business partnership of two different people, coming together to share resources, ideas, and friendship.

THOUGHTS

Be aware of people who cross your path and say yes to any meetings or get-togethers. You never know, you might just make a lifelong connection.

Three of Cups

It is one of the blessings of old friends that you can afford to be stupid with them.
—Ralph Waldo Emerson

Celebration, party, support of friends, pleasure, social contact, emotional happiness and joy

KEYWORDS

Celebration, party, support of friends, pleasure, social contact, emotional happiness and joy

Three penguins, each dressed in quite wacky clothing, appear to be having a party under the sea. Bottles of what looks to contain champagne, as well as cake, litter the floor below them. Two of them stand atop a dark sofa, one holding an umbrella (I mean, do you really need an umbrella underwater?!) and wearing a crown, and the other holding blue and green balloons. One penguin stands on the seabed, looking up at both of them. It appears as if they are all dancing and just being silly and finding joy in one another, strengthening their emotional bonds. How much have they had to drink? This is a beautiful scene of friendship, bonding, belonging, and getting drunk with your friends! We don't know what they are celebrating, but it appears as if it is a special occasion due to the champagne bottles we can see, and the cake. Is it a birthday, a graduation, a new contract or job, or even a hen-do (or penguin-do!). Who cares? It's time to overindulge, get your people together, put your glad rags on, and celebrate!

THOUGHTS

When was the last time you let your hair down? Consider arranging a party with your girlfriends or family. Surround yourself with people who make you happy, and have a grand old knees up!

Four of Cups

The opposite of love is not hate, it's indifference. The opposite of art is not ugliness, it's indifference. The opposite of faith is not heresy, it's indifference. And the opposite of life is not death, it's indifference.

—Elie Wiesel

KEYWORDS

Apathetic, disillusioned, antisocial, unmotivated, stagnated, lacking emotional satisfaction, fatigued, daydreaming

A wistful-looking mermaid sits on a swing above the water, looking down at the rocks. Mermaids live in the water, so why is she not down in the water instead of high up in the air, where she does not belong? A lamppost emerges from the sea, containing three lit cups, each representing an opportunity. A moon shines behind the cups, highlighting their glow. She, however, is not looking at them, preferring to be miserable. An upturned cup lies under her, facing to the left, signifying something that has passed. Is she focused on the fallen cup and the past, taking for granted what she does have but cannot see or appreciate? Is she bored? Or has she fallen asleep on the swing? How long has she spent on the swing asleep and missed many opportunities for happiness? She may be feeling stuck in a rut, not feeling able to get herself out of the despondency she is feeling. Perhaps feeling sorry for herself. She is unaware of the gifts being offered to her, due to her being indifferent. Her arms are crossed over her chest, almost as if she has closed herself down and is not open to letting anything into her heart.

THOUGHTS

If you are feeling down at the moment, feeling as if life has nothing new to offer, meditate and look at what has caused you to feel like this. Has something happened recently? Or do you just need some time to recharge your batteries? Plan a day for yourself, doing nothing but just chilling.

Five of Cups

Give sorrow words; the grief that does not speak knits up the o-er wrought heart and bids it break.

—William Shakespeare

Loss, bereavement, trauma, despair, grief, living in the past, isolation, loneliness, sadness

KEYWORDS

Loss, bereavement, trauma, despair, grief, living in the past, isolation, loneliness, sadness

A young woman, clad in a purple dress and floral headband, sits under a blossom tree, its pink blooms shading her and providing her with comfort. Something has really caused her immense pain—maybe it was a breakup, a divorce, a betrayal—whatever it was has completely crushed her. Beside her there are three empty cups, denoting what she has lost. The pain is spilling out of her, and she is distraught. She is not aware or is just not caring that there are two cups still standing upright next to her. She may have lost some things very dear, but yet there is still something of value remaining. The two upright cups may be assistance that is being offered to help her move on from this pain, but she is completely oblivious to them. Those cups are not going anywhere, and should she choose to see them, they will still be available to her. She is sitting down facing west, focused on the past, and is not quite ready to get up, turn round, and move on from the loss. There are small rock waterfalls in full flow to the side of her, suggesting that she is completely immersed in her grief. In time, she will look up and see the remaining two cups and take what they are offering, before moving on from this loss as a stronger person.

THOUGHTS

Is there something in your past or just now that you cannot move away from? Has something caused you pain that feels unbearable, and you seem stuck in the grief?

Six of Cups

*Remembrance of things past
is not necessarily the remembrance
of things as they were.*

—Marcel Proust

Nostalgia, sanctuary, memories,
reminiscences, childhood, past influences

KEYWORDS

Nostalgia, sanctuary, memories, reminiscences, childhood, past influences

A young woman, with long black hair and wearing a green hat, is sitting by the edge of a blue, shimmering stream. She is gently lowering six paper boats into six cups and letting them flow down the stream, reminiscing about the many fond memories she has of her childhood. All the while she is singing to herself, "Row, row your boat gently down the stream, merrily, merrily, merrily, merrily, life is but a dream . . ."

    Two clocks stand next to her. One is depicting the here and now, her reality as it is now. The other clock is running the time backward, her past, when she was a child playing with paper boats in the stream. A butterfly is hovering by the first clock, signifying that she is no longer the same person she was then. Butterflies are about transformation. It is letting her know that it is okay to visit the past and even allow yourself the memories, but the past is where it must stay. The boats and cups gently flowing down the stream are letting her know that right now is a time to just go with the flow and see where life ends up. In the distance, her present—her children playing with their kites, reminding her that much joy is to be had right where she is.

THOUGHTS

Is there somewhere from your past that you associate with happy memories? When was the last time you went there? Consider taking a trip down memory lane. Is it as you remember, or do you see it differently now that you are a different person?

Seven of Cups

Visualization is daydreaming with a purpose.
—Bo Bennett

Daydreaming, choices, fantasies, illusions, opportunities, procrastination

KEYWORDS

Daydreaming, choices, fantasies, illusions, opportunities, procrastination

In a blue, shimmering stream, there are seven swans, all minding their own business. Another swan is playing on a swing hanging from a tree while watching his two friends chatting away among themselves. Each of the swans in the stream is carrying a cup on its back, with a colored light glowing at the top of the cup. Each cup has an upright handle.

    We see a hand holding a fishing rod, with a hook attached to it. It is trying to hook one of the cup handles but seems undecided which cup he wants. Each cup signifies an opportunity, some of which are fantasies, which may or may not bring the person satisfaction, but he does not know which one he wants, so he just hovers with the fishing rod over the cups. Maybe he is feeling overwhelmed with all the choices available. He knows he will have to make a decision soon, since the swans will not stay still for long—they are swans and will swim off. Oh what does he do? Which cup shall he choose, or should he choose none and let the opportunities that are so available to him right now pass him by? He remains at the stream, daydreaming of what he will do once he has made up his mind.

THOUGHTS

What are your current daydreams? List at least seven, and which one will you take the step toward bringing to reality?

Eight of Cups

Your past is like a bag of bricks; set it down and walk away. Quit collecting every painful word, memory, and mistake. Collect hope.

—Bryant McGill

Moving on, breakup, walking away, leaving the past behind, abandonment, weariness

KEYWORDS

Moving on, breakup, walking away, leaving the past behind, abandonment, weariness

With her back to us, a woman with red hair walks through a large wooden door, through which we can see a bright light shining. Outside there is a darkness. A checkered path to the door is lit by eight cups, each emitting a glow, lighting her path to where she knows she needs to go. Situations from the past, represented by the cups, have led her to this point. The lessons have been learned, and she can do no more, so she allows them to show her the way forward. She is no longer in the darkness of uncertainty any more. A worn old suitcase lies in the middle of the path, as if abandoned by the woman. The burden of the heavy emotions she had carried for so long is now ready to be put down and left in the past, where it belongs. The tired, worn suitcase, representing her exhaustion, was dragging her down. It has taken all her strength to let it go and move on. A single red rose lies on the suitcase, which appears to be shedding its petals. The woman carries on walking through the door, never looking back. Dragonflies hover around the outside of the door, signifying the transformation the woman is going through, representing the clear insight that she now has to move forward into the light—to a brand-new future.

THOUGHTS

Ask yourself if you are who you want to be. If you are not, what is holding you back, and what do you need to let go of in order to be that person?

Nine of Cups

*Opportunities and choices.
When a person makes a heart wish,
that wish resonates through the
currents and things will happen to
give the person an opportunity to
make the wish come true. Like a hand
offered and accepted . . .*
—Anne Bishop

Wishes, satisfaction, happiness, dreams coming true, warmth, joy

KEYWORDS

Wishes, satisfaction, happiness, dreams coming true, warmth, joy

In a shimmery blue sea, a golden smiling Buddha, symbolizing luck, emerges from the sea holding a necklace of pearls adorned with nine glowing cups. It's almost as if he is saying, "Hey, look at what I just found!" Isn't he lucky? He is a jolly, happy chap, and his smile is almost as wide as his face, which is filled with sheer joy and pride. He looks completely satisfied. The moon is shining in the background, illuminating the sea and the Buddha. It's his turn to shine and be center stage for once. Fish and jellyfish swim around in the sea, his friends sharing his success. Later on, he will be sharing the cups—perhaps with wine—with his friends in the ocean, who supported him on his journey to this moment. He is the man who has it all. It's the moment he had been waiting for for a long time. He holds out the pearls and cups as if showing them off, and why shouldn't he? His riches have been hard earned, and he has had to go through many rough, emotional times to achieve his prizes. Each cup adorning the pearls signifies a victory over a hardship or heartache that he has overcome, which he will now wear with pride. His dreams and wishes came true.

THOUGHTS

What are you grateful for in your life? Spend some time looking at all the things in your life that you are grateful for. What would you like to attract more of?

Ten of Cups

No matter what you've done for yourself or for humanity, if you can't look back on having given love and attention to your own family, what have you really accomplished?

—Lee Iacocca

Security, happiness, domestic bliss, emotional stability, maturity, success

KEYWORDS

Security, happiness, domestic bliss, emotional stability, maturity, success

A warm, idyllic scene beckons us in the image. A sweet cottage home, lit with glowing lights, sits nestled among sheltering trees, in a garden by a gently meandering stream. Smoke slowly floats out of its chimney, suggesting a cozy warm fire inside. A couple sits embracing in the window. They appear to be watching something inside the house. Could it be they are watching their children at play? Whatever it is, they are showing a tender closeness. A sleeping dog lies in the lush green grass outside the house, safe in the knowledge that all is okay. Everyone is safe and secure, and life is just perfect. There appears to be nothing or no one to cause any upset or to be wary of. Outside, there is a bridge of ten glowing cups—each with a different-colored light—going from the garden to the other side of the stream. The bridge of cups is arranged in the shape of an arch, symbolizing it as a gateway to a new stage in life. The lights in the cups are lessons that have been learned over time, and they now light the bridge, providing it with the beautiful rainbow glows. The river shimmers in hues of blues and greens, as fireflies and dragonflies float on by. Beautiful flowers grow on the riverbank, injecting more color into this beautiful, happy scene.

THOUGHTS

Take a moment to look at who or what makes your life complete. How do you acknowledge that? If you don't, think of ways in which you can.

Page of Cups

I prefer to be a dreamer among the humblest, with visions to be realized, than lord among those without dreams and desires.

—Khalil Gibran

KEYWORDS

Message, love, dreamer, heart on sleeve, sensitivity, innocence, idealism

On a shimmery body of water, the Page of Cups sits in her small boat, on her way to deliver a message. The water looks calm—for now—but she is no stranger to being tossed about by the waves of emotions. She is adorned in a beautiful tulle white dress and has flowers in her hair, showing us that what she looks like matters to her. The moon shines brightly, giving her an almost ethereal, dreamy feel. A cup sits on a large shell in the water, and a small turtle pops its head out of the water, symbolizing a sudden idea or inspiration. The Page of Cups is a dreamer and struggles to remain focused. They are highly imaginative, and a lot of their time is spent with their heads in the clouds, making it difficult to get them to focus on anything for a length of time. They tend to deeply "love" something for a period of time, before discarding it for the next thing that catches their fancy!

Highly sensitive and artistic, the Page of Cups tends to feel things very deeply and has the ability to connect and feel the world around them, and because of this they demonstrate high levels of compassion. They go out of their way to show people that they care, whether it's giving them a cuddle or making something especially for them, because "you looked sad." They can be sweet little angels when they want to be. Because they feel so deeply, they may be prone to emotional outbursts, since they have not quite mastered the art of controlling their emotions. They do not know that emotions can be expressed in less harmful ways, and so they may come across as quite immature.

THOUGHTS

Take a look at the many unfinished projects you might have started. How can you revisit and continue with them?

Knight of Cups

Romantic, imaginative, sensitive, lover, knight, proposal, offers, seductive

'Tis better to have loved and lost, than never to have loved at all.
—Lord Alfred Tennyson

KEYWORDS

Romantic, imaginative, sensitive, lover, knight, proposal, offers, seductive

We see a garden at the entrance to what looks like the sea. Two pillars stand on either side of the entrance, and in the sea we see a young man, bare chested with a headdress of shells. He is holding a cup with a rose heart in his hand and appears to be offering it to someone who is out of view behind the right pillar. The moon is shining down on the water, and a floating island containing a lighthouse hovers in the air, shining a light toward the west. The Knight of Cups is a dreamy, sensitive, and highly emotional person. Is he offering the gift of friendship, or is the cup an offer of marriage? He is presenting the cup to the right of the image, in the direction he is facing, so is this someone he is looking to move into the future with? He does not appear to be looking at either the person or the cup he is offering, which can make us think that maybe he has not thought this through and is just offering for the sake of doing so.

He is a lover who can sweep any woman off her feet, and he does have the tendency to "fall in love" quite often. Maybe he has done this too many times before in the past—gotten involved only to lose interest. The lighthouse shining a light toward his past can suggest the broken hearts he has left in his pursuit of the "perfect" love, or that he himself has had his heart broken and has not fully dealt with past emotions. He may still be holding on to them, believing that creating a new future will erase the old wounds and the emotions he is clearly still submerged in.

THOUGHTS

Is there something that you have been dreaming of doing, of wanting to bring into existence? If so, what is the first step you can do to bring it alive?

Queen of Cups

When dealing with people, remember you are not dealing with creatures of logic, but creatures of emotion.

—Dale Carnegie

KEYWORDS

Loving, kind heart, intuitive, spiritual, psychic, healer, counselor, hormonal

The Queen of Cups lives deep under the ocean, submerged in her own emotions' feelings. Her beautiful clothing, created by materials from the sea, shows her ability to see and create beauty from the normal everyday things. She wears the sea, a place where she is the most comfortable. Her long hair flows behind her as she looks directly at the reader. She knows who you are, since she has the ability to penetrate deep into your heart and psyche, drawing out secrets that even you did not know you had.

In her right hand she holds a beautiful cup, showing her ability to hold deep love, both physical and spiritual. In her left hand she holds a trident, signifying her mind, body, and soul connection. She understands how the mind, body, and soul can be affected by extreme emotions, yet she still struggles at times to control them. She has a very highly developed intuition, which she needs to learn to trust more. The Queen of Cups has the ability to detach from reality, allowing herself into a world of imagination and dreams. This is where she escapes to when she is under pressure or stressed.

She is a dreamer and a visionary and thinks and trusts with her heart. Highly compassionate, she makes an excellent mother who is always there with a listening ear and a kind hug for her children's emotional issues. She has the ability to put herself in others' shoes and feel their problems, which makes her an excellent friend to have.

THOUGHTS

How often do you trust your own heart? If not, why?

King of Cups

Remember, NO ONE has the right to control your emotions, thoughts, and actions, unless you let them.

—Kevin J. Donaldson

Wisdom, calm, diplomatic, caring, tolerant, kind, gentle, emotional control

KEYWORDS

Wisdom, calm, diplomatic, caring, tolerant, kind, gentle, emotional control

The King of Cups sits on his shell-shaped throne under the shimmery green-blue sea. NO matter what is going on at the surface of the sea, he remains calm and controlled, his arms are folded to show who is in charge. He is surrounded by eight octopus tentacles, signifying his psychic ability and very strong intuition. The number eight is a symbol of abundance and prosperity, and this King is richly abundant in mind, body, and spirit. He helps others develop their gifts, without controlling them.

Sensitive, caring, and compassionate, he is someone who rules with kindness and grace. The tentacles show that he feels very deeply, and he is a ruler who is perfectly at peace with his own feelings and no longer feels the need to impress anyone—as he did when he was younger. He wears a crown, made up of different shells, echoing the headgear we saw in the Knight of Cups. This is the Knight who has matured, and as well as the shells, we see the King is wearing a tall hat on his head (a solid structure), signifying the control over his emotions. He has a large cup in front of him, signifying his wisdom. He contains everything he needs, and he knows intuitively what is required of him. He makes a great friend because of his understanding and is someone who you can turn to if you need honest advice.

THOUGHTS

How do you react to situations when they overwhelm you? Think of an instance when you felt overwhelmed and how your reaction affected the result. Looking back, what would you have done differently?

The Suit of Swords

Ace of Swords

Communication, clarity, breakthrough, truth, focus, justice, concentration, new ideas

The best way to succeed is to have a specific Intent, a clear Vision, a plan of Action, and the ability to maintain Clarity. Those are the Four Pillars of Success. It never fails!

—Steve Maraboli

KEYWORDS

Communication, clarity, breakthrough, truth, focus, justice, concentration, new ideas

A sword appears in the middle of the image, offering the gift of mental clarity, focus, and communication. Since it is upright, it offers the ability to see both sides of any situation, which is important in ensuring a balanced opinion to be formed. It appears to have shattered through glass, with shards exploding and flying around the sword. This signifies finally understanding the truth, shattering any assumptions and lies. There may have been a period of fog and confusion, but the sword has the ability to pierce through illusions, allowing clear vision. It cuts straight through to the truth. This is the moment of clarity, the breakthrough that has been waited for. The sword cuts through whatever is false effortlessly, allowing it to see the light. Lightning appears to strike the sword, indicating a sudden flash of insight, or a new idea that comes out of the blue, igniting ambition. Perhaps it is old beliefs and attitudes that are being destroyed by the lightning, allowing the space for new ones to form.

Swords are seen to be equipment that is a staple of kings and emperors. It is the weapon of taking charge and courage, and it allows its owner to take charge of their life and be the one wielding the sword. However, the sword, if it falls into the wrong hand, can cause untold destruction and pain.

THOUGHTS

What stops you from speaking your truth? What beliefs do you have that prevent you from doing so? Where do those beliefs come from?

Two of Swords

Life is full of confusion. Confusion of love, passion, and romance. Confusion of family and friends. Confusion with life itself. What path we take, what turns we make. How we roll our dice.

—Matthew Underwood

KEYWORDS

Confusion, choices, stalemate, closed heart, denial, head in sand, indecisive

The Two of Swords shows a woman with a hat covering her eyes. She cannot see where she is or what is around her, let alone in front of her. I she blind to her circumstances, or is she choosing not to see on purpose? Perhaps she covers her eyes so that nothing can distract her while she makes her choice. She sits on an ostrich, an animal known to bury its head in the sand. In her hand she holds two large swords, each pointing in different directions, two different choices, showing her indecisiveness in determining which way to go. She seems to be quite stuck and, instead of thinking with fear, needs to look at each option with a logical and rational mind, then pick one and get moving, or choose to remain where she is.

The lamppost behind her and the path is there to provide her with direction once she has decided to start moving, but she needs to be the one who makes that decision. She could continue to sit there forever, stuck on the ostrich, or she could get off and take the first step on the path behind her, heading toward the lights of the lamppost. Who knows, there may be even more markers from there, providing her with further directions as to where she needs to go. But right now, she is in a state of oblivion, the hat pulled down well over her eyes. The solution she requires is literally right behind her; it's very obvious, yet she is not willing to open her eyes to it. If she cannot see it, then it does not exist. Is she being stubborn? Does she not want to compromise, and is she standing in the way of her own truth?

THOUGHTS

If you have been struggling to make a decision and have been stressed by it, consider talking to someone else, since there may be a perspective that you cannot see.

Three of Swords

The worst pain in the world goes beyond the physical. Even further beyond any other emotional pain one can feel. It is the betrayal of a friend.

—Heather Brewer

KEYWORDS

Heartbreak, loss, betrayal, emotional pain, separation, sadness, trauma, tears

A floating blue heart of roses is pierced by three swords, indicating emotional anguish. The heart, which was once red, is now blue and cold. It has been hurt so badly that it has lost the color and life it once had. The heart is bleeding, except it is blue, cold blood. It almost looks as if the heart is turning to ice, creating an armor so that it can grieve. It needs to be mindful that it does not allow the armor to remain a permanent fixture; otherwise the swords will become embedded and difficult to move. The three swords are facing up, suggesting that the person, once they have grieved, will be able to see exactly what happened from each angle. It may also be that whoever pierced the heart was known to the heart; hence its complete shutdown. A horrible betrayal of the heart by people it trusted. It may be that more than one person was involved in the betrayal. The blue heart can signify that whatever it was may have come out of the blue, and the heart was not expecting it at all.

The heart is wearing a blue hat, with a chain attached to it. This signifies trying to cover up the pain, but it is too strong, and there is a need to think logically about what happened so that the pain can be understood and perhaps minimized. Also, there may still be something hidden that the heart is not aware of. It may be that there was a blessing in disguise that will reveal itself in time. The heart may have had a lucky escape, and although it feels as if the pain will never end, it might be grateful for the new information, and that may help it heal. For now, the heart will allow itself to grieve, before it blooms back into its beauty—for this too shall pass.

THOUGHTS

Think about a time in the past when you went through a major heartache. How did you cope, and what lessons did you learn at the time? Is there a hurt that you are still holding on to? What do you need to let it go?

Four of Swords

There is a time for many words, and there is also a time for sleep.

—Homer

Rest, exhaustion, retreat, recuperation, time-out, solitude, relaxation, sanctuary, peace

KEYWORDS

Rest, exhaustion, retreat, recuperation, time-out, solitude, relaxation, sanctuary, peace

A young woman dressed in blue clothing is lying on a tomb floating in the clouds. The swords are standing by her side, pointing down. They are her sufferings, which she has put to the side for now, allowing herself to not dwell on them. They have not gone away yet, since the issues are still there, but she is allowing herself a rest from them. She does not have the energy to deal with them right now, since she is completely and utterly mentally exhausted. She is floating in the clouds, far, far away from everyone and everything, the fluffy clouds providing her cushioning from all her pain. She holds one sword, laid across her body, ready in case she needs to suddenly awaken and fight.

A woman's face appears out of the right side of the image, facing the sleeping woman, who is in a deep meditative state. She is the guardian angel who is whispering to the sleeping woman, passing on clarity and wisdom to her as she sleeps, allowing whatever answers she needs to come to her as she "sleeps on it." The guardian angel will always be by the woman's side, letting her know that no matter what suffering she has in life, she can always come back to a restful state, where the angel will help her see and think clearly. She is her inner voice, the one that can be counted on when the mind becomes noisy. This inner voice cuts through the illusions and allows clear thinking and the ability to get to the truth of the matter.

THOUGHTS

When was the last time you heard yourself away from the hustle and bustle of daily life? Consider meditation or even a quiet sit-down in among nature to listen to what messages your inner voice has for you.

Five of Swords

Conflict, struggle, fight, aggression, defeat, bully, sacrifice, intimidation, abuse

Man is not, by nature, deserving of all that he wants. When we think that we are automatically entitled to something, that is when we start walking all over others to get it.
—Criss Jami

KEYWORDS

Conflict, struggle, fight, aggression, defeat, bully, sacrifice, intimidation, abuse

A young woman stands in front of some steps leading to a door, outside a woods covered in thorns. She wears a bright-yellow dress, the color of jealousy, and a very smug expression. In her hands she holds three swords, one held aloft as if in victory. Behind her sits a woman, kneeling down and crying at her loss. The three swords the other woman in yellow is holding were her swords. She was intimidated into handing them over. Two swords appear to be lodged in her back, because she stood up to the lady. It's her punishment for fighting for herself; she has been humiliated and brought down to her knees.

The woman in yellow looks very smug and satisfied. She knows what she has done is wrong, but her justification is that she wanted the swords, and she was going to have them at all costs. She won.

What she cannot see is that she may have won this little fight, but in the long run she may not have won at all. Word will get round that she had to bully another, and even more so, the fact that she had to bring the other woman to a quiet, secluded location to get what she wanted shows her underhanded, sneaky methods. One day she, too, may be stabbed in the back for what is hers. No one will trust her again, and she may even find herself isolated from others. She could still do the right thing: apologize and make amends with the woman she hurt with her cutting words, and give her back what she has taken.

THOUGHTS

Are you in an unhealthful situation in which you feel you are fighting a losing battle? What stops you from giving up and walking away?

Six of Swords

Better times, moving on, progress, calmer waters, healing, mental stability, transition

It happens to everyone as they grow up. You find out who you are and what you want, and then you realize that people you've known forever don't see things the way you do. So you keep the wonderful memories but find yourself moving on.

—Nicholas Sparks

KEYWORDS

Better times, moving on, progress, calmer waters, healing, mental stability, transition

A hooded, cloaked man holding a lantern and a staff stands in a boat, moving through the water. The water to the back of the boat appears misty and unclear, while the water at the front of the boat looks calm and still. The water signifies his emotions, which in the past were turbulent and clouded his judgment. The water appears much calmer indicating that he is able to see clearly and think rationally, rather than letting his emotions control him. He has had to endure some very difficult times, which can be seen with the six swords that are in the boat with him, signifying the stressful situations he has had to deal with. Tthey are facing down, so they are no longer a threat. He has overcome the situations that pained him, forever carrying the lessons and wisdom they offered.

The boatman carries a lantern emitting a blue light. Blue is the color of the throat chakra, which denotes speaking your truth and honesty. He carries his truth with him and trusts that it will steer him to where he needs to go. He does not have anyone else in the boat with him, indicating he is not controlled by the opinion of others. HE determines where he is going.

The boat is heading toward a gateway, signifying he is in a period of transition and has not quite reached his destination. So there may even still be a few more trials left, but he must ensure he stays the course and does not give up. He is almost there, and the worst is over!

THOUGHTS

Consider taking yourself away from a troubling situation to get some distance to think it through.

Seven of Swords

Deception, treachery, lies, enemy within, theft, cheating, sneakiness, plotting

Oh, what a tangled web we weave
... when first we practice to deceive.
—Sir Walter Scott

KEYWORDS

Deception, treachery, lies, enemy within, theft, cheating, sneakiness, plotting

A woman wearing magpie wings, a face mask, and golden feathers in her hair is kneeling by a tree. In front of her lie six swords, which she seems to be hoarding. A seventh sword lies behind her, almost as if she dropped it and is unaware it is there. A magpie wearing a tiara is sitting on a branch next to her, holding a pearl necklace in his beak. The woman is looking shiftily at the magpie. What if he decides to raise the alarm, since it seems she has been caught?

A window is behind the woman, indicating a building of some sort. Has she taken the swords from the building behind her and, in her rush, dropped one of them? Perhaps she thought she might get caught and thus ran away, not noticing the dropped sword. Why is she dressed like the bird? Is she hoping that if someone saw her taking the swords, they would think it was a magpie and not her? Or perhaps the hoard actually belongs to the magpie, and she is now claiming it? Perhaps the magpie thought she was a friend, but all along she was only pretending, so she could gain information to deceive him. Whatever she is trying to do, it appears to be very sneaky and underhanded. She has her hand over the swords, which indicates she is trying to hide what she is doing, but the swords are quite large, and although a part of them may be hidden from view, they are still visible.

A dreamcatcher is attached to another branch above the woman, signifying the night, when everyone is asleep. It acts as a web where the bad dreams are caught in the center of the web, allowing the good dreams to flow down the feathers to the person dreaming. Is the woman about to be caught up in the web of deceit that she appears to have spun?

THOUGHTS

Think of a situation you might be in where you cannot seem to find a solution. Is there something that you may be overlooking?

Eight of Swords

You feel powerless only because your fear has given your power to the object of your fear. Once you realize this, you can claim it back.
—Kamand Kojouri

KEYWORDS

Restriction, indecision, confusion, confinement, trapped, powerless, depressed, paralyzed

In a wintery forest, a cloaked woman is standing by a tree. She is blindfolded and her hands are tied up, although it appears the binds are almost breaking. She does not know how she got here, yet here she is. Eight swords surround her, almost like a prison. Is this a prison of her own making, or is she caught up in someone else's? She may have trapped herself due to her own thinking and is afraid to move. There is a very clear gap in the swords for her to move forward and escape should she choose to. However, since she is blindfolded she cannot see that the ribbon binding her wrists is frayed, and if she wants she can break it and remove the blindfold. This would allow her to see the gap and walk away from the situation that encircles her. She appears almost resigned to the fact that she is trapped, and it appears as if she is choosing not to free herself from the binds. She may be so used to the situation that she is in that she no longer can identify with being trapped. She has given her power away to another in the situation, allowing the prison to be the only thing she knows, and perhaps she even finds a familiarity and comfort in it. She may believe that she has no option but to remain where she is, because if she moves, she will be sliced to bits. Oh, if only she could open her wrists and break the bonds.

A baby deer is sitting at her feet. The fawn symbolizes the peace and love that is waiting for the woman once she rips off the blindfold. It is waiting patiently to remind her of her strength, no matter how frail she may be feeling right now. She will survive this and she will get out of this situation, and he will help her along her path with fearlessness. Until then, he will wait.

THOUGHTS

Today, look at something where you may be feeling trapped. Are you really trapped, or can you do something about it? What is stopping you?

Nine of Swords

You learned to run from what you feel, and that's why you have nightmares. To deny is to invite madness. To accept is to control.

—Megan Chance

KEYWORDS

Nightmares, despair, guilt, depression, anxiety, fear, negativity, mental anguish

Nightmares, despair, guilt, depression, anxiety, fear, negativity, mental anguish

A woman sits on the floor, leaning against a pillar. Her right hand covering her eyes as if she is crying her eyes out. A dragon's head appears out of the image, with its mouth wide open, and yellow, glowing eyes. He has nine swords coming out of his head, as if they are a part of his appearance, and a full moon is shining behind him. The swords signify the world she has created in her mind. The dragon is her "mind monster"—her fear. If only she would remove her hand and see that everything around her is not real, as indicated by the full moon. She has allowed all her fears to emerge into the conscious. If she were to look closely at the dragon, she would see that it is almost transparent, indicating he is not real.

Bats fly above the dragon's head, adding to her fear. A clock is sitting on the floor, indicating she has been in this situation for a very long time. It is held by a ghostly apparition. This apparition represents someone who is close at hand—whom she cannot see—and can help her out of her worries. Roses bloom at the bottom of the image. She has allowed this situation to bloom into being, and since the roses are creeping over the bottom of the image, it is not too late to prune them back before they grow and take over the entire situation. A web hangs above the woman, again signifying she is trapped in her own self-induced nightmare and paranoia. She has allowed her fear to take over and become so huge that she believes the worries to be larger than what they are. Perhaps she has ignored them for so long that she no longer knows how to get herself out of the situation.

THOUGHTS

Think about a problem you may be facing in life just now. Is the problem really as bad as you think?

Ten of Swords

When you feel like you have been hit, dig deep and hit back. Rock bottom is not your end; it is your beginning.
—Christine Evangelou

KEYWORDS

Rock bottom, pain, loss, abandonment, backstabbing, martyrdom, collapse, failure

Rock bottom, pain, loss, abandonment, backstabbing, martyrdom, collapse, failure

A woman with closed, crying eyes is holding a sword. Nine other swords are lodged in her back. She wears an eyepiece on her left eye and could have seen what was coming. The one sword in her hand indicates that she tried to fight whatever her situation was, but since it is facing down, not much of a fight was put up. She knows that the swords that are piercing her will drain the blood from her eventually—unless she can pull them out. How much does she want to live?

She is looking back at the castle that is visible through the window behind her, signifying that she had it all, and now she stands distant from it, alone and distraught. Everything has ended, causing her emotional pain. The swords are stabbing her in the back, indicating that she was running away from her situation and that if only she had faced them head on, then she would have been able to see them and deal with them with clarity, honesty, and wisdom. Or maybe she was stabbed by someone she trusted, and she is crying because she now sees them for what they are.

There is a light shining on her from one of the windows, so not all is lost, showing her that even this dark night will have a dawn and that she will be able to start anew, should she choose to. The decision rests upon her. Is she going to continue in her "poor me" self or is she going to stop crying and follow the light that is beckoning her, and begin again, having learned from her mistakes? If you look closely, you can see that the swords in her back are not too deeply embedded, so she could put down the one in her hands, pull out the ones in her back, and move on. Not all is lost, and sometimes new beginnings come disguised as painful endings.

THOUGHTS

Is there anything weighing you down? Imagine what your life would look like and sound like if you released them.

Page of Swords

The most important thing in communication is hearing what isn't said.

—Peter Drucker

Written message, communication, ideas, information, inspiration, direct

KEYWORDS

Written message, communication, ideas, information, inspiration, direct

In front of a balcony with floaty white curtains stands the young Page of Swords, wearing a blue dress and cloak. The blowing curtains may indicate an approaching storm, yet she stands unfazed, carrying a large sword and looking as if she is ready to strike if needed, with a look of defiance and determination on her face. No storm is going to stop her on her mission. She wears a headdress of wings and a blue tiara. She is fast and swift, which can lead her to be impatient and rash, preferring to listen to herself and not to others. She may leave you as quickly as she arrived, preferring not to hang around. She requires constant stimulation and needs to learn to be a bit more patient and not rush things. As a page, she lacks the maturity to understand this. A lantern glows behind her, and there is a full moon in the sky.

The Page of Swords brings messages that may not be as they appear to be; there may be small print that is covered up among the rest of the message, indicating they might be deceptive. Ever ready with their sword, they may pass on messages that are really gossip and misinformation. They love to communicate (even argue for the sake of it), and hey, passing on gossip is communication—right? She is the news bearer, bringing messages of perhaps legal matters, contracts, or conflicts, which require you to be alert and remain sharp.

THOUGHTS

Today, look at something you want to try but are too scared to do, in case you mess it up. Consider doing some research and gather info before creating a plan of action.

Knight of Swords

One of my weaknesses is impatience. I just have this aching need to get great things done. Can't stand slow change.
—Robin S. Sharma

KEYWORDS

Fast moving, impatience, rash, fearless, brave, daring, direct, going against flow

The Knight of Swords, wearing her armor, is heading into battle, wielding her mighty sword. Behind her is a fast-moving river that appears to have flooded the woods. The knight does not seem bothered by that and is confidently forging ahead. The knight really needs to be aware of what is going on around her, so that plans can be adjusted as new information comes to light. A plane flies overhead, heading into the opposite direction of the Knight. There are lightning strikes in the sky, and it appears as if the plane is trying to get away from them.

The lightning strikes are indicating a serious and quite intense situation that is forming, which has the potential to cause major disruption. This may happen suddenly and quickly, and the Knight may have to change direction and take charge quickly before the situation escalates.

The Knight of Swords is a very rash and impulsive person, and we are left wondering if this chaotic situation is their own creation. They are known for their love of "shaking things up." Are they heading off to fix the situation, or are they going into battle, as we originally thought? Perhaps they are leaving the scene of chaos, and the plane up in the sky is the rescue squad, coming in to survey the damage and clean up the mess the Knight of Swords has made.

THOUGHTS

If there is something you want to do and you want to do it NOW, then take the first step, pause, and look to see if there is any other information before you take the second step, rather than jumping in headlong.

Queen of Swords

She holds herself with such reserve. She smiles, but the smile doesn't reach her eyes, even in the company of the girls she's chosen to eat with.

—Lauren Myracle

KEYWORDS

Quick witted, independent, honest, principled, intellectual, aloof, divorced

The Queen of Swords looks out with a cool, calm expression with no visible emotion. She wears a magnificent crown of ice and cold blue, wearing her aloofness with pride upon her head. Her long hair, with hints of an icy gray, flows down her shoulders, signifying the wisdom she has earned through her journey. Having overcome a great deal in her life she now has the wisdom to pass it on. The fact that she allows the gray to show and has made no attempt to cover it up indicates that she does not care about the opinion of others.

There is a sword in front of her, covering her heart. She puts the mind over emotions in any decisions that she makes, and for this she is known to be a just and wise Queen who is as decisive as she is quick. Very direct and to the point, she says it as it is, even though it can come across as aggressive or hurtful to hear what she has to say. However, if she feels injustice is being done, then she will not hesitate to fight in your corner.

Sshe works alone, without anyone's input, or it may be that she is divorced or widowed and as such has gotten used to dealing with things on her own. Perhaps her sternness and aloof nature are because she has had to hold the fort on her own, and to prevent people from manipulating her or taking advantage of her. She does not want to let anyone close to her, so the facade of being cold helps.

THOUGHTS

How do you communicate? Are you direct and to the point, or do you have a tendency to beat around the bush?

King of Swords

The man who passes the sentence should swing the sword. If you would take a man's life, you owe it to him to look into his eyes and hear his final words. And if you cannot bear to do that, then perhaps the man does not deserve to die.

—George R. R. Martin

Maturity, authority, clarity, judge, analytical, principles, reason, logic, power

KEYWORDS

Maturity, authority, clarity, judge, analytical, principles, reason, logic, power

The King of Swords, with his blue clothes, a symbol of authority, and his deep-blue, ice-cold eyes, looks right at us. He rules with logic and reason. He wears a tall hat, with a white crown sitting on it. His tall hat represents structure and stability. Structure and routine in life is important to him. He too has a sword that is covering his heart, meaning emotions play no part in his decision-making. He logically analyzes any issues before he arrives at a conclusion. The sword in the middle of the image shows all sides of an issue before coming to a balanced decision.

His white hair signifies wisdom that has come with age and also a reserved exterior that he portrays to others. He needs to ensure he remains unemotional if he is to rule wisely. It does not mean he is completely unemotional; he is, it's just that he has learned to master his emotions and be in control of them, rather than have them running riot and controlling him.

Behind him some birds are visible flying over the forest, signifying that as King, he knows he may need others to gather and provide him with information. Ultimately, he sees the bigger picture and makes the decisions.

THOUGHTS

If you are in a situation that is making you emotional, clear your mind and try to be objective. What comes up?

The Suit of Wands

Ace of Wands

Believe in your infinite potential. Your only limitations are those you set upon yourself. Believe in yourself, your abilities, and your own potential. Never let self-doubt hold you captive. You are worthy of all that you dream of and hope for.

—Roy T. Bennett

Energy, inspiration, pregnancy, passion, creation, spark, potential, optimism

KEYWORDS

Energy, inspiration, pregnancy, passion, creation, spark, potential, optimism

A wand is emerging from a field of sunflowers. The wand is brightly lit by the sun behind it, glowing bright yellow, symbolizing a powerful creative energy. Shoots emerge from the side of the wand. Each shoot contains a lantern, which is unlit, indicating emerging ideas and possibilities that have not yet manifested fully into the physical. They are just untapped opportunities. Sparks of inspiration and passion flow around the wand, which are required to ensure the shoots flourish and grow. Ideas cannot bloom if there is no passion or energy behind them. Perhaps a new job or business is being offered. The sparks flying around the image are ushering in exciting times. Things may be heating up for you in some area of your life.

The large sun behind the wand is suggesting that the future is bright. The field of sunflowers is offering endless joy and success if the moment is seized. If it is not, then the shoots will wither away and die, leaving behind missed possibilities.

The wand stands tall above the field of sunflowers, suggesting there is the possibility to reach great heights as long as limits are pushed. There are no limits to reach for the sky. There is a chance to pursue a dream that is being offered by the wand, a golden opportunity to express creativity. Will it be accepted?

THOUGHTS

If life has been dull and boring recently, think about what you can do to inject a spark of life into it. What would you love to see happen?

Two of Wands

Choices, a fork in the road, decisions, indecision, pause, timing, planning, taking the first step

Faith is taking the first step even when you don't see the whole staircase.
—Martin Luther King Jr.

KEYWORDS

Choices, a fork in the road, decisions, indecision, pause, timing, planning, taking the first step

The Two of Wands features a woman dressed in a bright-green dress wearing a red hat. In front of her are two staircases, each lit with a glowing wand. A golden compass hangs between the two staircases. By her side is a red dragon, looking up at the compass. Both of the wands appear to be lightly placed at the foot of the stairs, indicating their lack of stability. They could be moved at any time, since they are not rooted in the earth.

It appears the woman has a choice to make. Which staircase should she take? Both would lead to different options, as indicated by the light levels on the staircase. She seems almost stuck and cannot make a decision. The compass is pointing to the right, yet she does not know if she can trust the compass. Perhaps both options are okay, and each will lead to different outcomes. How will she know unless she takes the first step and moves?

The dragon by her side may be someone she is planning to go into partnership with, or it may even be her inner guidance that is telling her to trust the compass. Trust that whatever path she takes, it will be the right one for her at that time. There may be an option to change course farther down the way, but right now, this is the best way for her. Or she could remain where she is. She needs to stop waiting for someone else or something else to happen, and to trust in herself and make the first move. She needs to find that passion and inspiration that fuels her. There is a huge world and unlimited success up there that beckons her, and if she wants to make her dreams come true, that isn't going to happen standing at the bottom of the steps.

THOUGHTS

Take time out today to look at how far you have come, before looking at where you want to go. If a next step presents itself, then trust your instinct and go for it!

Three of Wands

A ship in port is safe, but that's not what ships are built for. Sail out to sea and do new things.

—Grace Hopper

KEYWORDS

Confidence, expansion, growth, foresight, waiting, shipping, commerce, exploration

A woman stands on a balcony, looking out to the sea and sky. Her back is to us, indicating she is not looking to the past but to what lies ahead, allowing her to see any issues that might be appearing over the horizon, so that she is not caught off guard. There is less chance of any surprise attacks if she can see far. Three airships fly in the sky, and some appear to be leaving the shore, while others are coming in. Some may have been gone for a very long time, and she has had to have patience awaiting their return, along with the rewards they bring. Or perhaps she turned away an opportunity in the past, and it is now coming back to her again. Will she accept it this time around?

A large red planet is visible in the sky, representing new, undiscovered lands waiting to be explored. New opportunities are on the horizon. She stands there holding three lit wands, to help the airships coming back from the red planet, wondering what exciting new cargo it will bring her. These will bring her new opportunities, and she might even expand her business in a new territory, with people who are different from her.

One of the airships has a rope ladder that has been lowered. Is she going to seize the opportunity to jump on and see where it takes her? Is she willing to go fearlessly where no one has gone before, and have the courage to follow her heart? Perhaps this is her chance to leave what she knows and go exploring in order to ensure rewards. Who knows what she might discover and learn along the way? She does not want to stay still, and three wands are facing in different directions, meaning she is ready to move in whichever way her heart desires. There are no restrictions.

THOUGHTS

How often do you take a risk and move out of your comfort zone? What prevents you from trying something new?

Four of Wands

Remember to celebrate milestones as you prepare for the road ahead.
—Nelson Mandela

Celebration, marriage, community, stability, parties, reunions, domestic bliss

KEYWORDS

Celebration, marriage, community, stability, parties, reunions, domestic bliss

A festive wedding canopy supported by four lit wands in each corner stands in the center of the image. It is a solid stable structure that has been built on reliable foundations. Roses and ribbons adorn the top of the canopy, signifying passion and love. Decorative, glittering white lights dangle down from each corner of the canopy, almost like a waterfall of sparkles. A man and woman dressed in wedding attire are making their way into the canopy. They look as if they have just gotten married. Brightly colored flowers mark the entrance to the canopy, and there are butterflies flitting around above it. A full moon shines on the happy couple, adding to the glow of the happiness that can be felt from them.

They are on their way to celebrate their union with their family and friends, since they could not have done it without them. They have reached a milestone in their life and are wanting to acknowledge it with the people who matter. Much more work needs to be done, since this is just the beginning. The openness of the canopy suggests there is nothing standing in their way, and there are no secrets between them. Having their back to us suggests they are moving away from whatever restrictions or limitations they had in the past, and they are celebrating as they move away from it. There is a strong bond between the two of them as they hold each other's hand. They are walking together hand in hand toward a new phase of life. To a new period of growth and happiness.

THOUGHTS

How often do you acknowledge and celebrate the good times in your life? Next time something great happens to you, get together and share your success with your friends and family. Don't keep it to yourself!

Five of Wands

A quarrel is quickly settled when deserted by one party; there is no battle unless there be two.
—Lucius Annaeus Seneca

KEYWORDS

Competition, conflict, fights, battle, challenges, strife, disagreement, hassle

The Five of Wands shows five lit wands encircling a group of stags, who appear to be fighting or challenging one another. Sparks are flying all around them, suggesting passionate and fiery conflict. Each of them appears to be carrying something different on their antlers, suggesting their individuality. They are each different from the other yet cannot see that their differences can be utilized to bring about successful outcomes.

It could be that one of them feels more important than the others. They each want to be the leader, leading to a lot of aggression and bad feelings in the group. No one wants to listen to each other, and they are all against one another. The items that each one is carrying may be obstacles that they are putting in the way to prevent the others from becoming successful. What they don't realize or cannot see is that continued fighting will only lead to destruction and failure. The sparks that are flying between them may eventually turn fierce and destroy them all. They need to make sure each one of them can communicate his needs in a calm, compassionate way and allow others to voice what they have to say, instead of everyone arguing at once.

It may be that each one of the five stags represents the many critical voices of one person. The voices may be fighting with one another to be heard. It could also indicate that there are a lot of issues happening at the same time. Each issue needs time to be resolved, instead of trying to fix them all at once. Perhaps there is a situation that needs to be resolved, and because it has a lot of people involved, everyone is just going around in circles!

THOUGHTS

Are you at odds with anyone in the workplace or at home? Are you really listening to them, allowing them to voice their concerns, or do you get all defensive?

Six of Wands

Triumph, accolades, pride, victory, recognition, success, glory, admiration

It is better to conquer yourself than to win a thousand battles. Then the victory is yours. It cannot be taken from you, not by angels or by demons, heaven or hell.

—Buddha

KEYWORDS

Triumph, accolades, pride, victory, recognition, success, glory, admiration

A large gold medal hangs by a green ribbon in the center of the image, signifying pride. Its owner is very proud of its achievements. The medal contains a large sunflower at its center, with large sunlike beams bursting out of the side of the golden disc. Six wands are placed at the bottom, each wand lit and adding to the glow of the medal. The medal is being showered by golden confetti, showing that the recipient is adored by many who think they are amazing. They should bask in the glory for it belongs to them.

The medal is located in the center of the image, symbolizing that the recipient is loving their time being center stage. Why should they not be in the limelight for once; they have earned it, after all. This is a moment of victory and of beating all odds to be triumphant. The recipient has been recognized. They have succeeded and others are now applauding their success or victory. The wands at the bottom of the medal suggest that it was not an easy victory, and a lot of hard work went into this successful moment. They have won gold, not silver or bronze, which means they have had to beat off stiff competition. They are enjoying the moment but must keep in mind that while today this medal and this success belong to them, their competitors are watching and waiting. In the future, this victory could be snatched out from right under their nose, so they need to ensure that they carry on building on their success and not just think, "I have made it." Success is very fickle—here today, gone tomorrow! Enjoy it while it lasts.

THOUGHTS

What does success mean to you? How will you know you have "made it"? What will it look like and sound like?

Seven of Wands

Trust your own instincts, go inside, follow your heart. Right from the start, go ahead and stand up for what you believe in. As I've learned, that's the path to happiness.

—Lesley Ann Warren

KEYWORDS

Conviction, defiance, defensive, courage, perseverance, tenacity, determination

A woman dressed in green stands on top of stairs in front of a large closed door. She holds a wand, the top of which is glowing very brightly. On either side of the door are lit candles, and there is a clock on the right pillar. She has lost track of time and does not know how long she has been standing there defending herself. At the bottom of the steps, six wands are pointing toward her. The tops of the wands are burning with flames. They are challenging her, trying to scare her with the fire so that she will move from her position. There are many of them and only one of her. The woman has a look of defiance on her face. She is not moving as she tries to defend her position, holding her ground. It feels like everyone is against her, but what if they are not? What if SHE is the one who needs to change her perspective? It's all very well having convictions and being prepared to fight for them, but what if they are not justified?

She is standing above them, meaning she has chosen to rise to the occasion, and since she has the higher ground, she knows that she is right to make a stand. Her wand glowing brighter than anything else in the image shows the passion behind her convictions. She will stay true to her integrity and will not compromise. It may be that she is fighting on behalf of someone else. Is there something or someone behind the door that the challengers wish to take over, and she is not letting them? It may be someone who cannot stand up for themselves, someone who society thinks should be hidden away, and so this woman is being their voice and fighting for their rights.

THOUGHTS

How often do you back down just to keep the peace? Have the courage of your convictions to say no the next time you want to assert yourself.

She was like a bird for speed, an arrow for directness.
—Virginia Woolf

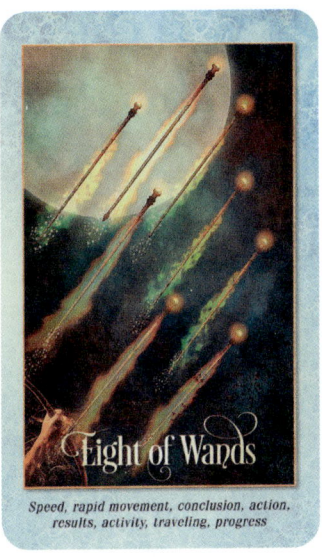

Speed, rapid movement, conclusion, action, results, activity, traveling, progress

KEYWORDS

Speed, rapid movement, conclusion, action, results, activity, traveling, progress

Eight lit wands fly thorough the air, like fireworks, each one having come from a bow seen at the bottom left-hand corner of the image. Each wand flies past the large moon, seeking its target. They have been fired and will not stop now until they have reached their goal. Each wand represents a sudden burst of energy, which will move the archer forward at speed. The wands, once shot out of the arrow, are expected to gain momentum very quickly, so if something had been stuck for ages, it will suddenly start moving again, and very quickly, so there must be no hesitation to grab the opportunity when it arises.

It may look as if the wands are "up in the air," suspended and not moving, but they ARE moving. They may be taking their time to get to the target, since they may have great distances to travel, but they will reach it in their own time. Nothing can stay suspended in the air—it is not physically possible. It may be that some of the wands might fall short of the target and not quite make it, but that is okay. The ones that are meant to be will hit the bull's-eye no matter what. The ones that don't were not relevant. The wands may represent desires or thoughts that have been sent out to the universe, where not everything that is wanted is manifested, only what is needed.

THOUGHTS

Consider what it is that you would like to manifest, and send an intention out to the universe, without any obsessive need for it to appear in a certain way. Watch and wait.

Nine of Wands

Nothing can dim the light which shines from within.
—Maya Angelou

KEYWORDS

Weary, last stand, perseverance, determination, courage, inner strength

An exhausted-looking woman stands holding her wand for support. She would probably collapse if the wand was not there. There are broken pillars around her, wiht cracks in the stonework of some of them. Much has been destroyed in her quest. What was not destroyed has left a scar but still intact, symbolizing that the woman's strength and courage have not been destroyed, just wounded. Standing behind her are eight tall wands, dimly lit, depicting the trials and tribulations she has undergone and left behind. They may even be the battles she has already won. They are in her past and she has come through them. Each of them has left a mark on her, depleting her energy, but showing her an inner strength she did not know she had. She is nearly at the end, but is too tired to fight today. She is alone and she is aware that whatever final stand needs to be taken, she will have to do it on her own. So, for now, she will allow herself to rest, reflect on what happened, and replenish her strength so that she may carry on.

The end of her ordeal is not far away; there may be a final trial or tribulation to go before she reaches her goal, which is the final wand that she is facing at the moment. In the image, she is standing almost at the end of the scene, which denotes it is nearly the end of this chapter. She still has some fire and strength left in her, as symbolized in the glowing wand she now rests on. This is the very fire and strength that got her this far. She will dig deep into the reserves of the inner strength she possesses, and will achieve her goal. She may feel like giving up, but as long as that fire burns she is not going to quit!

THOUGHTS

If you have exhausted yourself trying to reach a goal, consider taking some time out and rethinking your strategy.

Ten of Wands

Burdened, struggling, duty, obligation, responsibility, stress, weighed down

People become attached to their burdens sometimes more than the burdens are attached to them.

—George Bernard Shaw

KEYWORDS

Burdened, struggling, duty, obligation, responsibility, stress, weighed down

A woman is kneeling in the grass, on the ground in front of a gate. She is weighed down by a large rock she is carrying. The rock is tied to her waist, and the burden of it has brought her to her knees. Ten wands are also in the pack that she is carrying, some brighter than others. It seems that she cannot get up—the burden is too heavy. She has worked so hard for this, and right at the end she is struggling. The gate, her destination, is so close, yet due to the load she carries, she cannot see where she is going. She seems to have lost sight of the goal. There may be one final push required, where all she needs to do is to turn around, see the gate, and enter. She knows that if she can get her bundle through the gate, then she and others will be able to reap the harvest that was planted many moons ago. She does not want all that effort to have been in vain.

It seems the woman has taken on more that she could possibly carry, and perhaps what once gave her satisfaction has lost the excitement and become a burden, denoted by the varying degree of glows emitting from the wands on her back. Their fire has been dying, yet she still carries them. They have now become a burden, and she feels obligated in continuing to carry it. Perhaps it is time to let them go. The obligations are as heavy as a rock. The wands represent the ideas, jobs, projects, etc. that she began in full faith of seeing them through to completion, but she lost interest in them along the way. She may consider passing on some of her responsibilities to another, who may be able to inject life back into them, while she carries on the ones that will reap stronger rewards for her.

THOUGHTS

Consider if there is something that you once were passionate about and you now carry. Is it weighing you down? What stops you from laying it to rest?

Page of Wands

*Never allow anyone to define you!
Just be you!*

—Chrys Phillips

KEYWORDS

Exuberant, outgoing, excited, creative, artistic, free spirit, original, inventive

A young Page of Wands is wearing a gold glitter hat with gold feathers, on his head. A peacock feather is displayed quite proudly in the hat, signifying happiness and lots of new divinely inspired ideas. The peacock is normally seen as a vain bird who uses its feathers as a grand display of vanity, just like the Page of Wands, who loves to be seen. He likes nothing better than being the center of attention. His clothes certainly aren't those of a shy, retiring wallflower. They scream "look at me," and he is not someone who would want to blend in to the background! The sunflower shows us that he is a very happy, optimistic soul with a lot of love and warmth for others. Two pocket watches dangle from his hat, indicating that he has much to learn and that there is still a lot of time for his ideas to materialize.

From his attire, it is quite clear that the Page of Wands is a highly creative person, and the fiery colors in the image show us his excitement and passion. He is the fire that sparks the creativity of big, grand ideas and of excitement at pursuing those ideas. His message is to think big and just go for it, no matter how unique or way out there the vision may be. The Page of Wands is full of energy but may be a bit scattered with it, beginning new projects with a grand burst of excitement and then losing interest down the road. He would rather spend time daydreaming on the grandness of the project and what it will look like when it's finished, rather than do the work. He would rather be out partying or having adventures!

THOUGHTS

What excites you? What can you do to bring some fun and spark into your life?

Knight of Wands

If you think adventure is dangerous, try routine. It's lethal!

—Paulo Coelho

Brave, travel, energy, risk taker, adrenaline, daring, wanderlust, sudden, rebel

KEYWORDS

Brave, travel, energy, risk taker, adrenaline, daring, wanderlust, sudden, rebel

The Knight of Wands, sits on his motorbike, ready for action and battle. In his hand he carries his shield as protection against the dragon flying up ahead. Not that he thinks he needs it. He is daring, he is brave, and, of course, he is going to vanquish the dragon and return home as the dragon slayer, and they will all tell tales of his heroics! But what is he going to kill the dragon with? A wand? Hmm . . . doesn't look like our Knight of Wands really thought things through. He heard about a dragon that needed slaying, and off he sped. He had time to put on his armor, but forgot to pick up his sword. The wand is not really going to help him, is it? If only he had stopped and taken the time to create a plan!

The Knight of Wands enjoys the thrill of a grand adventure, and the rush he gets feeds his body and soul. He is, however, quite impulsive, and many a time he has jumped into something believing he knows it all, only to jump straight back out, leaving a mess (and broken hearts) in his wake. The Knight is not really the most dependable, being constantly on the move—here today, gone tomorrow!

This Knight loves being in love. It is all grand gestures and passion, but remember what I said about him being impulsive and jumping into things? Look, what's that over there? Something else that's shiny and new; of course he just HAS to go explore it! But wait, what about you? Well, it was fun while it lasted, wasn't it?

THOUGHTS

You may be stuck in a rut. What can you do to shake things up a bit? Go exploring, have an adventure. Anything to break the routine!

CUT TEXT

Queen of Wands

Whatever you do, be different—that was the advice my mother gave me, and I can't think of better advice for an entrepreneur. If you're different, you will stand out.

—Anita Roddick

KEYWORDS

Dynamic, energetic, creative, visionary, entrepreneur, optimistic, extrovert, dramatic

The Queen of Wands stands facing out, with her back to a richly adorned red-and-gold throne. She is not sitting on her throne. That is what is expected of a Queen. But she is different. She cannot think of anything worse than sitting on her throne, day in and day out. Where is the excitement in that? Boring! She is dressed in a bright-yellow kaftan, symbolizing her exuberant warm personality and the sign of Leo, a fire sign, the element of the Wands. Lions' heads are emblazoned all over it. The lions represent her fearlessness, strength, and courage. They also nod to her wild and untamed side, a side that is sometimes covered under the myriad of daily responsibilities. It is always there, and she is not afraid to show it when required. She is matriarch of her kingdom. Her hair is tied up in two large knots, and on her head she wears a gold crown with a red ruby in the center. Behind her stands a tall wand. Her face is heavily made up with stunning makeup. She looks gorgeous and she knows it—she does not need anyone to tell her.

She is bold, fiery, passionate, cheerful, and energetic, and there is nothing she loves more than keeping busy and socializing. How else is she going to get a chance to show off her amazing beauty? She is a natural extrovert. Very confident in herself and her abilities, she has deep inner strength to bring her ideas to fruition. A highly independent woman, she may run many successful businesses (always the leader—not the follower). Her fearlessness at standing up for the truth may find her fighting on behalf of those with no voice. She is fierce in her fights and would go to the ends of the earth for a cause she believes in. You certainly would not want to mess with her!

THOUGHTS

What new goals can you set for yourself? How can you use the energy of the Queen of Wands in developing those goals?

King of Wands

There's more to being a king than getting your way all the time.

—Mufasa

Leader, vision, inspiring, energetic, moral, fair, mentor, bold, dynamic

KEYWORDS

Leader, vision, inspiring, energetic, moral, fair, mentor, bold, dynamic

The King of Wands stands by his grand throne, half man, half horse, representing the fire sign of Sagittarius, leading the charge with his new ways of doing things. He is in great shape, a result of many hours of various fitness activities. This is a King who is not afraid to be different, to challenge the old ways. He holds a guitar in his hand, showing his love for music. After a hard day of ruling, he likes nothing better than to unwind with a few tunes. Like the rest of his family, the King of Wands likes being center stage, and he certainly does not lack in confidence, as shown by the sun crown on his head and etched into his throne. He is a fearless leader, leading with compassion and charisma, and people respect him.

Persistent and focused, he will keep going when others have given up. Once he has set a goal, then he wants to achieve it. He is not afraid to show others who is boss, yet at the same time he has the ability to inspire others to reach great heights. He knows that true power lies in helping others see theirs. He believes in them, and so should they. A highly principled man, he is a tolerant leader until his principles are violated, or if he doesn't get his way. Then he can become a sulky toddler. The King of Wands is an extrovert and loves being around people, making a great host. He is the life and soul of a party, and you know he is in the room since he exudes a radiance that only a King of Wands can. Very caring and genuine, he would give the shirt off his back to help someone who needed it (hmmm, maybe that's why he has no shirt on in the image!).

THOUGHTS

How often do you feel in control of your own life? If you don't, then why not, and what do you need to do to be back in power?

The Suit of Coins

Ace of Coins

Plant seeds of happiness, hope, success, and love; it will all come back to you in abundance. This is the law of nature.

—Steve Maraboli

New financial beginnings, new job, opportunities, abundance, wealth, investment, windfall

KEYWORDS

New financial beginnings, new job, opportunities, abundance, wealth, investment, windfall

On the entrance of an open door, there lies a wooden chest containing a large gold coin. The coin is gift-wrapped in a large red bow and ribbon. There is a label attached to the chest, simply stating, "For you." The gold coin in the chest is the gift of a new material beginning from the universe. Red roses tumble out from the side of the chest, and a large, beautiful peacock sits on top of the coin. The peacock (a bird of beauty) is looking toward the right of the image, signifying things to come. Should this gift be accepted, then there is a beautiful future awaiting the recipient, provided he takes care of the coin and invests it wisely. There is nothing else showing who this gift is from. A large tree with lush green leaves stands behind the chest, and it appears this is a scene in a richly fertile forest. Pink flowers glow at the entrance of the doorway, adding to the beauty of the image.

The forest and the flowers are showing that all seeds require time and patience to grow, and although there is a single coin in the chest, it can be turned into many. For that to happen will require sensible investments and patience. The investment will need to be nurtured with time and energy for it to yield an abundant harvest. Or it can be spent straight away and squandered, with nothing to show for it. It is an unexpected gift, a new opportunity, or even an inheritance, which has the potential to bring huge abundance and many opportunities. It is the foundation on which great things may be built.

THOUGHTS

If you have been considering changing careers or starting a business, then this may be a good time to take the plunge, as long as you remain grounded and methodical.

Two of Coins

Fortunate, indeed, is the man who takes exactly the right measure of himself and holds a just balance between what he can acquire and what he can use.

—Peter Latham

KEYWORDS

Juggling finances, choices, cycles, spinning plates, cash flow, money stress

Juggling finances, choices, cycles, spinning plates, cash flow, money stress

A woman stands on a unicycle, which is balanced on a piece of cord or rope. Her arms are outstretched, and in each hand she holds a gold coin, one of which is higher than the other. These could signify time, money, resources, or even her thinking. Is she giving too much importance to one thing over another? The infinity symbol curves around the two gold coins, showing her constant readjustment, trying to find the perfect balance with them, ensuring she doesn't drop either of them or herself. Her dress is made of red feathers, and on her head she wears a tall brown hat. A red curtain hangs at the left side of the image. The color red corresponds to the root chakra, which is concerned with the basic requirements to survive and feeling grounded. The woman is balancing in the air, on a rope, and is far from being grounded. She knows she needs to get back down to earth, back onto solid ground, and that is exactly what she is trying to do. At this time, however, she is trying very hard to make ends meet, perhaps financially. She may be juggling finances by taking from one place to pay another, or perhaps she is working two jobs, which is leaving her with a feeling of exhaustion.

The curtain on the left hand side of the image symbolizes her fear of the "curtain coming down on her"—the end of everything she has been working for, possibly even financial ruin. For now, she appears to be managing just fine and to be keeping calm among the pressure of keeping the balance. She is aware that remaining calm and collected will get her to stability.

THOUGHTS

Take a look at what is happening in your life, and identify areas where you may be giving out more than you are getting. What strategies can you implement to ensure things are more evenly balanced?

Three of Coins

Individual commitment to a group effort—that is what makes a team work, a company work, a society work, a civilization work.

—Vince Lombardi

KEYWORDS

Teamwork, assistance, asking for help, mentors, apprentice, learning, study

Three flying ants are making their way to land in a patch of forest, where many hundreds of other ants are proceeding toward a hollow in a tree. There is a golden glow coming from the hollow. Each flying ant is carrying a gold coin. A lamp hangs off the tree, emitting a green light, directing the flying ants to the rest of the team. Red toadstools adorn the forest, bringing a pop of color into the image.

The ants on the ground look really busy, carrying stuff. It looks as if something beautiful is being created in the hollow, and that all the ants are playing their part in the creation. Each one is bringing their own unique skill to the construction. The flying ants bring the skill of oversight, since they are responsible for the practical planning and strategizing of the work that is going on. From their vantage point, they can see anyone who is struggling, and are able to assist them, perhaps even mentor them, until they are confident enough to go it alone.

Everyone appears to be working hard; the ground is a buzz of activity. They all know that hard work now will mean they get to enjoy the fruits of their labor later on. In the image, all the ants are heading in the same direction, indicating a common purpose. Ants are a very hardworking insect, and they work as a team. Each ant in a colony has its own specific task, its own specialities, and each one knows exactly what needs to be done and when. Despite their size, ants have the ability to accomplish great things. They work together for the benefit of their team, and it's their focused effort that makes the team thrive.

THOUGHTS

What new skills would you like to learn? Consider expanding your skill set by researching new courses. Sign up for them.

Four of Coins

*The miser is as much in want of what
he has as of what he has not.*
—Publilius Syrus

Possessiveness, control, selfish, miserly, hoarder, insecurity, frugality, greedy, rigid

KEYWORDS

Possessiveness, control, selfish, miserly, hoarder, insecurity, frugality, greedy, rigid

In a richly decorated room, a woman sits on a chest of her possessions. Many open chests filled with expensive jewels and money lie around the room. She is dressed in very expensive clothing, and in her arms she holds on to four gold coins. Her posture is very defensive and almost aggressive. Plush curtains hang on the window, which shows a view of bare trees. Two lamps are lit on either side of the window, and a lantern is by her feet. Behind her is a small squirrel who seems to be hiding coins behind the hem of the woman's dress.

This is a woman has worked very hard to ensure she is financially stable. Because the coins cover her heart, perhaps she had to sacrifice her emotions to get to her position. She may have been a workaholic, with no time for matters of the heart, and now it remains guarded. She has squirreled away enough to keep her in luxury, but she is afraid that one day she may lose it all, so she is holding on tight to what is hers. What if someone steals it during the night? "I know," she thinks, "I will spend my nights in the room, so no one can come in and steal from me." She is holding on tight to the coins and from the look on her face is not prepared to share with anyone. She needs to relax, since the full chests around her show that there is plenty to go around. By holding tight, she is only blocking further abundance from coming in, since her actions are telling the universe she doesn't have enough. The gold coins may represent a person, feelings, or even a secret that she wants to hold on to. Perhaps a relationship has outlived its purpose, but she has a fear of being on her own and is happy holding on to something that no longer serves her, or maybe she did let go and is now holding on tight to the past.

THOUGHTS

How efficient are you with finances? Do you spend, spend, spend, or have you made plans for a rainy day?

Five of Coins

Five of Coins
Financial hardship, homelessness, abandoned, downcast, loneliness, isolation, struggle

Overcoming poverty is not a gesture of charity. It is an act of justice. It is the protection of a fundamental human right, the right to dignity and a decent life.

—Nelson Mandela

KEYWORDS

Financial hardship, homelessness, abandoned, downcast, loneliness, isolation, struggle

A woman in rags sits outside, with her back to a grand entrance. Five gold coins adorn the entrance. She has as her processions an unlit lamp and a hat that is lying upside down on the ground beside her. The woman looks sad and is looking at the ground in front of her. She once had all she ever wanted—riches, love, possessions—until one day, everything just came down on her. She lost it all and was evicted out into the cold, with the bare minimum of her possessions. The lamp offers no light since she cannot afford the fuel, signifying that her inner light has gone out, and she sees no way to relight the passions that once fueled her. Her hair is messy and unkempt. She feels completely and utterly alone, abandoned to the elements.

A hand emerges from the right side of the image, throwing coins into the woman's hat, offering help. She is unaware of this help as she stares straight ahead. She may be on the streets, but pride is stopping her from asking for help, so she hides her face in case anyone recognizes her. She does not want people to know her situation. Shelter and help are always at hand, and if she were to turn round, she would see the coins displayed on the entrance, offering stability, help, and perhaps even food. She could knock on the door and have shelter and the opportunity of a new start, but she chooses to remain where she is, unaware of all the help around her, lost in her misery.

THOUGHTS

If you are struggling with managing your money, research what assistance is available to you. Perhaps you need an accountant or some other financial institution to help create financial plans.

Six of Coins

When we give cheerfully and accept gratefully, everyone is blessed.
—Maya Angelou

Charity, exchange, benevolence, handouts, welfare, sharing, generosity, assistance

KEYWORDS

Charity, exchange, benevolence, handouts, welfare, sharing, generosity, assistance

A large, golden-colored set of balance scales is sitting in the woods. The woodland is very rich and green, indicating abundance. Two plates make up the scales, with one plate slightly higher than the other. A hand reaches out of the right side of the image, and it looks as if a gold coin is being placed onto the plate. A hand also emerges from the left side of the image, and it looks as if it has just taken a coin from the plate. A total of six gold coins are visible in the image. A red ribbon is entwined around the bottom of the scales, indicating the provision of basic needs.

The scales represent sharing, with the gold representing money, time, or emotions. The hands giving and receiving denote the need to be balanced and not to give too much away, so that the other plate is then depleted. The giving and receiving needs to be balanced and fair, since only when balanced do the scales represent fairness. At the moment, the scales do not appear to be balanced—there is more on one plate than on the other. Perhaps the giver is giving away too much of themselves emotionally and is not getting the same back in return? Perhaps the recipient is not being appreciative and has taken too much, to an extent that the giver is now becoming depleted and does not have much more to give.

The lush woodland, the ornate balance scales, and the shiny gold coins all indicate someone who is financially very secure. They can afford to give knowing that life is an endless cycle of giving and receiving. They are generous and are willing to help someone else who may be in need.

THOUGHTS

Think about the number of times you may have had to share something. Did you do it out of your own free will, or was there some agenda behind it? What do you possess that you are willing to share, without any expectations of a return?

Seven of Coins

Nature herself does not distinguish between what seed it receives. It grows whatever seed is planted; this is the way life works. Be mindful of the seeds you plant today, as they will become the crop you harvest.
—Mary Morrissey

KEYWORDS

Harvest, patience, reward, perseverance, results, dividends, progress, profit

A bright-red harvester sits in the middle of a field, its lights on. In front of it is a tall crop consisting of seven gold coins, which can indicate money, relationships, or time. There is no one on the tractor, which signifies that although the crop looks ready, it has not quite matured, and therefore patience is required before it can be harvested. The farmer is at home, having a rest after all the hard work that went into growing the crop. The seed that was planted a few weeks ago has now borne fruit, but it requires just one final wait. The farmer has patiently waited so long, working hard, in all types of weather and all hours, persevering with feeding and watering the fields. He is so close to success.

The crop containing the seven gold coins is in the center of the image, and every shoot has borne fruit, indicating pride of place. Once harvested, the fruits of labor will ensure a time of financial improvement for the farmer and his family. He needs to remain patient, because if he pulls out the crop before it is completely ready, he will destroy it, and all his hard work will be worthless. He can use this moment in time to take a break and reflect on what he is going to do next. Since all the seeds have sprouted, he might even consider taking only what he needs and investing the others, to ensure an even-bigger crop next time around.

THOUGHTS

If you have been working hard recently, and it's felt like work is all you do, consider taking a well-earned break. What will you do?

Eight of Coins

There are two men inside the artist, the poet and the craftsman. One is born a poet. One becomes a craftsman.

—Emile Zola

KEYWORDS

Apprenticeship, craftsmanship, hard work, craft, discipline, meticulous, pride, specialist

A beautiful stained-glass window is visible in the middle of the image. It is surrounded by lots of green leaves, denoting abundance. The window is painted in greens, yellows, reds, and orange colors. Eight gold coins surround the window. This window is perfection, and it looks as if it has been created by an expert craftsman. A lot of focus and hard work have been required to get the precision that is evident in the creation. Perhaps this is the creator's first accomplishment on his own. Maybe he was an apprentice to a master from whom he learned the intricate techniques. The beautiful flower in the center of the window signifies the love that has gone into the work. This may be something the craftsman enjoys doing, and it no longer feels like work to him.

  He has taken his time to make sure even the smallest areas are painted, making sure all the details are correct and nothing looks out of place. Perhaps he is a perfectionist. It must have taken a long time to do, since the window is set among the leaves of trees, which could have been distracting. He may have had to spend long periods where he was not comfortable, especially if painting the window required many hours up a ladder. He would have had to remain focused and dedicated to the task in hand, ignoring the distractions around him. Because of his hard work, and success on this project, he may now find new jobs and opportunities arriving his way, which will allow him to use the experiences and lessons he has learned.

THOUGHTS

What things are you good at? Is there something you can teach others and perhaps make some extra income in the process?

Nine of Coins

*Opulence. You own everything.
Everything is yours.*

—Paris Is Burning

KEYWORDS

Luxury, abundance, wealth, success, independent, opulence, thrive, comfort

A stunning woman with long black hair cascading down her face looks out of the image. She wears a wreath of rust- and green-colored leaves, with a pair of stag's antlers, perfectly balancing nine glowing gold coins. Peacock feathers, associated with luxury and vanity, adorn her hair, and she wears a beautiful necklace of diamonds and rubies. She wears a tiny nose ring and ruby jewel on her forehead. The nose ring is signifying the association of the Coins suit with the Earth sign of Taurus. She remains grounded and down to earth. She is at one with nature, as seen by her associations with the leaves, antlers, and feathers. Her dark-green eyes stare straight ahead. This woman is opulence, and she is showing it off too!

Everything the woman wears belongs to her, and her alone. She has worked hard and the autumnal leaves show the many seasons that have passed and how long she has had to wait for her rewards. She is probably the owner of at least one, if not many, businesses and has expensive tastes. She is wearing a lot at one time, which may indicate someone who can be quite extravagant. She is alone in the image, which shows her independence. She has gone out and gotten what she wanted, and she hasn't waited on someone to provide it to her. She hasn't needed a man to provide for her, as shown by the antlers—she is the perfect balance of male and female energies, which has played a part in ensuring her success. She is very grateful for all she has achieved, since she knows that nothing lasts forever. For now, she is grateful for her blessings and going to just take her sweet time and enjoy it all.

THOUGHTS

How often do you feel grateful for the blessings in your life, or are you taking them for granted?

Ten of Coins

Carve your name on hearts, not tombstones. A legacy is etched into the minds of others and the stories they share about you.

—Shannon L. Alder

KEYWORDS

Home, family, stability, security, inheritance, legacies, reputation, affluence

It is Christmastime, and there is a beautifully decorated tree in the corner. A log fire casts warmth and light into the room. A wreath hangs over the large fireplace, which is richly decorated with garlands. Ten gold coins hang down from the garland. Presents and toys are lying on the rug in the room, adding to the overall festive scene. One present contains the same label that was seen on the chest, at the Ace of Coins, when a gift was left at the doorstep of an old wooden door. Could it be the same one? An armchair sits next to the warm fire, a place to sit and admire the fruits of the success.

The owner of this room is not to be seen. Perhaps he has gone to the door to receive his guests. It is Christmastime, after all. A time to celebrate with good food, wine, and the company of the people who matter, whether they are friends or family. Presents will be exchanged, and the present with the label will be passed on to someone else, for whom it will provide abundance—just like it did to the owner, all that time ago. The ten coins over the fireplace show that the owner has plenty of wealth to share and hand out, most likely to his children and grandchildren. He has much, and it is time to pass it on to the next generation. The coins may represent traditions, or a business that is being handed down, or may mean actual money, in the form of inheritances. It may even be assistance to help another's business get started. The owner has been through the path of hard work to arrive at his current status. He may now be using his business wisdom and knowledge to help someone else at the beginning of their journey.

THOUGHTS

Think about the legacy you wish to leave behind. What will it look like and sound like? What can you do to begin creating your legacy?

Page of Coins

Studious, nurturing, grounded, dependable, scholarly, prospects, diligent

When the student is ready, the teacher will appear. When the student is truly ready, the teacher will disappear.

—Tao Te Ching

KEYWORDS

Studious, nurturing, grounded, dependable, scholarly, prospects, diligent

A very young Page of Coins stands in what appears to be a library in the woods. A white ruffled collar covers his neck, signifying purity and his innocence. To the side of him lies another pile of books and a scroll, on top of which a large gray owl sits, staring with his round yellow eyes. His round eyes mimic the round glasses on the Page of Coins. Foliage climbs up the corners of the image, suggesting the fertile Earth. Behind the boy is a gold round clock. Glowing dragonflies and butterflies fly around the top of the Page's head, suggesting it is evening and signifying that learning does not stop when the sun goes down.

The Page of Coins is a young student who is about to begin learning his trade. The wise owl represents his mentor, from whom he will learn. The books by his side and behind him contain all the knowledge he needs to ensure a secure future. Through these he will learn how to plan and utilize resources to ensure success. He will learn that success comes from hard work and by being level headed and grounded, as shown by the abundance of nature. He has his tool—the pen tucked away—and is ready to begin learning.

As a messenger, he brings news and messages related to financial stability, such as a new job, a promotion, or even letters of acceptance from universities/colleges. The Page of Coins is someone who is well balanced, practical, and grounded and may be the class geek and a perfectionist. They are slow to react, preferring to take their time making a decision.

THOUGHTS

Think about a new project that you are wanting to start. How prepared are you?

Knight of Coins

I thought, I need to be more cautious about my choices—it reflects on who I am.

—Heath Ledger

KEYWORDS

Cautious, reliable, grounded, serious, patient, stable, traditional, disciplined

The Knight of Coins stands by his beautiful brown horse, looking in the same direction. They appear to be in woodland, with glowing dragonflies flying by the side of them both. The Knight wears an armored helmet, and a red cloak is covering him. He wears a gold coin around his neck, and there appears to be one in the center of his helmet too. He carries no sword, indicating he is not there to fight. Neither he nor the horse is moving. He is assessing the situation, and if he feels he needs to go into battle, then he will go away and draw up battle plans. He will do it properly: assess, plan, assess again, and then, only if necessary, will he pick up his sword and attack. The Knight of Coins is a very cautious man who moves at a snail's pace. Slow and steady is his mantra. He does not believe in rushing into anything, and people around him can get frustrated at his speed. Like a stubborn horse, once he has made up his mind he will refuse to budge, so the best thing to do is to step back and let him take his time. Just accept that this Knight will think before he acts. Things will get done when he is ready to move. He believes in going with the flow. Highly dependable, he is extremely hardworking and trustworthy. He is happy plodding along, reaching financial stability in his time, no matter how long it takes. Grass may grow under his feet before he even thinks about moving!

The Knight of Coins is very much connected to the Earth and nature. The red of his cloak indicates being grounded and rooted. It's where he feels most at home—in among the trees and animals.

THOUGHTS

Consider and research any books or audios that may enhance your career or relationship.

Queen of Coins

Be the one who nurtures and builds. Be the one who has an understanding and a forgiving heart one who looks for the best in people. Leave people better than you found them.

—Marvin J. Ashton

Mother, Earth, feminine, homemaker, compassionate, nurturing, generous

KEYWORDS

Mother, Earth, feminine, homemaker, compassionate, nurturing, generous

A beautiful woman sits in the forest, surrounded by plants and blossoming flowers. On her head she wears the most stunning tiara of gold leaves, the center of which consists of a shining golden coin. Her head is further adorned with a crown of branches and flowers, signifying her deep connection to nature. The branches consist of many pink blossoms and lit jewels, like fairy lights, in vibrant colors. Her long chestnut hair cascades down her shoulders onto her red dress, the red signifying her being grounded to the Earth. A hummingbird is approaching her. She looks out of the image with a very serene, peaceful look on her face. She is Mother Earth. She is the Queen of Coins, and all the rich colors around her denote her success and prosperity.

The Queen is known for her generosity and compassion. No matter who comes to her, whether at home or at work, she makes time to listen. She is sympathetic and kind, providing a warm, nurturing mother energy to those who need it. She is a homemaker, with family very important to her. She enjoys organizing the environment around her, so that her family can be comfortable. The Queen of Coins is earthy, calm, grounded, wise, mature, in possession of good instincts, and trustworthy. She is not someone who gives too much sway to flighty ideas; her motto is to keep it real!

She loves helping people but may find herself at times doing too much, even sacrificing her needs for the needs of others. Because of this she can sometimes develop a martyr complex.

THOUGHTS

What are ways in which you might be able to provide security to those closest to you?

King of Coins

Do whatever you want to persevere, work for your own things, and do not depend on anyone to be your provider. That way, in the future, you will be all right regardless of the circumstances.

—Dascha Polanco

Mature male, businessman, provider, master, successful, father, reliable, boss

KEYWORDS

Mature male, businessman, provider, master, successful, father, reliable, boss

The King of Coins stands proud and tall at the entrance to his kingdom. He is surrounded by lush greenery, showing material abundance and financial security. He is dressed in a rich coat of golden yellow, a color associated with the solar plexus chakra. This is where self-esteem resides, and this King exudes self-confidence. He knows who he is and is very secure in himself. He wears a necklace of pearls with a large red ruby at its center, signifying his wealth. He has worked very hard to achieve all of his wealth and status. On his head he wears a gold crown, which is decorated with antlers and lush green leaves. This shows his connection both to nature and animals. In front of him sits a hawk, staring straight ahead. The hawk is a bird of prey that can fly high and see situations from various perspectives. They symbolize the ability to focus, lead, and influence others—all qualities that the King possesses.

The King of Coins is a measured, practical, and quite conservative man who likes to do things in his own time. He usually advises people to check all the paperwork, especially the small print, so you know exactly what you are getting into. Earthy and solid, this is a King who loves the outdoors and may be involved in some sort of business that is linked to nature. Perhaps he can enjoy the outdoors since he does not need to work as hard anymore. He has made it and can enjoy the fruits of his labor while other people work for him.

THOUGHTS

What are your priorities in life? Where would you like to be in five years' time?

Acknowledgments

There are a few people whom I want to thank as this deck comes to life.

First and foremost, I want to give a huge thanks to the wonderful director of REDFeather Mind, Body & Spirit Publishing—Chris McClure, for his amazing encouragement and appreciation of my work, which has allowed me to bring this deck to the public via his team. His faith in me inspires me to keep creating, and I want to thank him for that (and I think he has gotten the message by now—I hate writing!)

Also, my gorgeous daughter, Amber, who has helped create some of the wonderful stories of the Major Arcana. I hate writing (I think I mentioned that before), so I enlisted the help of my journalist daughter to assist me, and she has done an amazing job . . . so thank you, Amber.

Other people I want to thank are my family and friends and my other children [Aaliyah and Arran]).

A HUGE thank-you to the lovely Ellen Wolfson Valladares, who not only is my soul sister but also helped edit the Major Arcana stories, since I am pretty hopeless at such stuff. Ellen is also the cocreator of the *Hummingbird Wisdom Oracle Cards*.

I want to thank my lovely friend Kalliope Haratsidis, for telling me the lovely story of the three sisters and the Wheel of Destiny—much appreciated.

To the team at REDFeather, especially Carey Massimini (for my constant questions!) and Peggy Kellar, my editor, with whom this is my third deck, after *The Tarot of Enchanted Dreams* and the *Hummingbird Wisdom Oracle Cards*, for yet again doing an amazing job and bringing my vision to life.

And, finally, to all you wonderful people who have bought the deck and who appreciate my work . . . I thank you from the bottom of my heart and soul. Welcome to the *Tarot of the Enchanted Soul*.

All my love,

Yasmeen Westwood is a self-taught photomanipulation artist living in Perthshire, Scotland. Her first deck, *The Tarot of Enchanted Dreams*, was released in December 2019. She was a finalist for her artwork, for the MPower, Mums in Business National Business Awards 2019, and was runner-up in two categories of the International Tarot Foundation CARTA Awards 2019 (Best Illustrator of a Tarot Deck and Best Self-Published Tarot Deck). In 2020, she won the Coalition of Visionary Resources (COVR) Bronze Award in the Tarot Deck category for *The Tarot of Enchanted Dreams*.